Author: Keith Deutsch

Preface

The Myth of Sisyphus

French philosopher, Albert Camus, won a Nobel Prize in 1944 for his work on the absurdity of the human experience. But unlike most of his contemporaries, Camus proposes that at the end of the day, our hero must be happy. This was a completely new idea in 1944. Before Camus's insight, those who studied classic philosophy were led to one of two undeniable and inexorable truths: that due to prevailing and predominate chaos, either the logical conclusion to existence has to be that the only control we have is to kill ourselves or not, or that we are ultimately controlled by some external creator force, and that implies that there is no choice or control at all.

The model of the absurd hero was outlined by Camus in his description of King Sisyphus. Sisyphus was the King of Corinth and the King of cunning. He had a silver tough and a love for the experience of life. Perhaps he loved life too much. Realizing that, he took full advantage of his position as King. The story tells that Sisyphus would take the wives of his politicians for his bedmates, and he was even involved with a plot to kill his brother. Not a morally sound individual, but he would have found the idea of morals completely unnecessary. Once he realizes the absurdity of the world, he realizes literally all its absurd opportunities; and along the way, that life has no meaning. That without comparison to each other, there is no scale or place at all for any kind of assumed morals. This leads him to the idea that "What counts is not the best living, but the most living."

The fact is that most would have viewed Sisyphus as a villain. But he saved everyone's life by making all of humanity immortal. So, he was, a hero. You see, the story goes that Sisyphus was able to trick the reaper himself into a set of chains in the underworld. While the reaper was trapped, all of humanity became immortal, saving the entirety of humanity from death. However, in this story, we are left to wonder if he did it to save humanity, or if he just wanted the fame.

Sisyphus was eventually discovered, and the gods were upset. As a punishment, Sisyphus was condemned to push a large boulder up a hill every day for eternity, and at the end of each day to see it roll back down giving him a task to begin anew the next day. This is a metaphor for the state of being each of us experience everyday as we "push our own rocks." The metaphor is a beautiful one. But the most beautiful part of the story is that Camus concludes that Sisyphus must be happy. That in life, pain is inevitable, but that suffering can be optional.

As I continue the story, Sisyphus keeps pushing his rock each day along the same path. This goes on for some time and eventually he makes friends along the way. One day, his friend tells him a story about his own past that helps give Sisyphus hope for the future. Once he discovers hope, his perspective changes. Now that he has hope, he stops suffering. Hope equals control, and just like that, Sisyphus realizes that he had won his immortality. All he had to do was push a silly rock every day. That didn't mean that's all he could do or that he wasn't allowed to enjoy it.

I like to picture Sisyphus polishing that rock and boring three holes in it. Then, at the end of each day, letting a different friend push it down the hill, where before he left in the morning, he left ten pins set up to aim for. Eventually he called this new sport, "bowling."

What follows is the story of a rock so big it took many to push it. It's a story of courage and compassion. It's the story of a mother, who stands by the side of her son, even though many days the rock seemed like it was too difficult to push. It's the story of a young man who is influenced by the many friends he encounters as he pushed his rock every day. It's the story of a father who wants to pass lessons he's learned on to his most precious gift, his daughter. Hopefully like Sisyphus, this story will give you a different perspective on life, a perspective filled with hope in your future and empathy for those you encounter along your journey pushing your own rock. I hope to inspire you to be the hero of your own story.

Chapter 1

My late Dad, Ron Deutsch, was a lifelong skier. And I guess I must give Dad a lot of credit for the influence he has had on my life. Even though snowboarding was not yet an option for him, his passion for skiing impacted me even as a youngster. Although the Deutsch family farm is in south central Minnesota, Dad had gotten a good taste for skiing while he and Mom lived in Colorado. They decided that after college, but before they had kids, they would move out west in order to see and experience more of the country before they settled down on Dad's family farm for the rest of their lives. Mom says Aurora, Colorado was the fastest growing city in the country in that day, and that is where my oldest sister, Jessica, was born. Dad was a bike mechanic and would earn a management position quickly at a shop called "Aurora Honda." I think the shop is still there today.

From the first time that I heard Dad mention it, I could see on his face that he was extremely excited when he talked about skiing. However, after decades in the Midwest, he talked about skiing almost like a mid-westerner would. "Bombing the hills," with little need to turn; was my entire view of the sport before I experienced the actual mountain at Big Sky as a preteen years later. Dad was fearless on the hill, and he wanted to show and share that which he loved with us, his 5 kids.

I can recall our family's first trip to go skiing. We drove for hours to the middle of Wisconsin. If I remember correctly, Righ, Wisconsin was known in the 80s for their great skiing, so "Christmas Mountain" was our destination. However, it was no mountain. In fact, it may not qualify as anything other than a bunny hill when compared to a Colorado slope. I was on skis back then, just maybe 8 years old. I don't remember much about most of that trip, although I do remember a lot of kids sleeping in one bed.

There is however, one thing that stands out clearly. That evening, Dad led my sister, Jessica, and I out to the lift. I'm not sure if we planned on this being our last run or not. Winter "snow," in the Midwest means ice, always and only ice. Ice is a fast and technical surface to ski on. Jessica was first up the lift. The seat only held two, and Jess was old enough to ride on her own, so Dad rode with me. Now, if you know Midwest skiing, then you know that the hills we rode were short. Unless there was a turn, we could always see the bottom from the top. If I didn't turn, I could be to the bottom of the hill by the time the next chair unloaded; being literally the only one on the hill. That is just what Jessica did that evening.

As the lift started to slow, I remember hearing Jessica's scream. I remember the tone in her voice like I remember the cries of men in war. However, at the time, I didn't realize the impact of it.

I was chuckling, and I remember saying to Dad, "It sounds like Jess is having fun."

But the look on Dad's face was severe, and he was already down the hill by the time the lift operator stopped the lift to help me off. As I pizza'd down towards where Jessica lay crying, I couldn't help but notice that she was twisted up like a pretzel; screaming in a tangled pile. There were lots of tears and cries, my Dad's, and her own. Dad yelled at me to get help, but I didn't need to. Everyone on the hill had heard my sister already, so there was no need for me to get involved. As I got closer, my pizza turned to French fries. Dad yelled at me again, this time in a cautious tone, "Stay back! Don't come any closer!" Even from a distance, I could work out what had happened. Jessica hit some ice, one ski went one way and the other went another. I'll never forget her scream. In fact, it brought me a tear when I first recalled it again and wrote about it. Jessica got a cast that went all the way up to her hip, and it remained that way for months.

At 8 years old, it was already utterly obvious to me that skiing was inherently dangerous, because your legs could go in any direction. I'm pretty sure it was right then that I decided to snowboard instead of ski. If not right then, I am sure that that was a strong motivating factor.

This was still the late 80s. If you can't remember that far back, bangs were huge, but snowboarding wasn't. Although it had been invented already decades earlier, it would still be a few years before the likes of Jake Burton, Tommy Sims, and the, "original gimp" himself, Lucas Grossy, would start to build the sport of snowboarding into what it was to become.

I do believe that the evening that Jess broke her leg was the last day that I considered myself a skier, and it was likely my last day ever skiing, with two legs anyways. I understood that what happened to Jessica could all too easily happen to me, so I decided quickly after that, that I wasn't going to ski. But at the same time, I had already realized a lifelong passion for sliding snow. I was addicted to the speed and sense of freedom that the hill afforded me. From the first time I saw the look on Dad's face and then slid snow, I was hooked. My love for it was passed down directly from Dad. It was as inherent in me as my brown eyes. I wouldn't learn for years what that would eventually mean to me; but at 8 years old, not only was the seed planted, but a path to Colorado had already been lit.

As the next few years passed, we didn't ski much, but my family was active in our YAC group (Young Active Christians). My parents' YAC group took a winter trip to visit a friend of ours every year. He was a priest named Fr. Denny. All the YAC families stayed together in this huge house or hall, probably a convent. This is where I met some of my first friends.

One year, my friend, Eric Goodman, and I both got snowboards for Christmas. They probably weren't what you're thinking of quite yet, however. Mine was called the "Black Snow." It was an all plastic, mono-directional, edgeless, green and black monster with a single strap to hold my feet in place. The harder you kicked your feet into the strap, the more likely they were to stay in place to the bottom of the hill. Eric's was similar, and we rode them happily for years. We weren't any good at it yet, but we didn't have two digits in our age yet either.

Dad got sick again when I was 8 or 9. The cancer came back metastasized and everywhere all at once; from his brain to his skin to his spine and liver. Bumps were visible all over his body as the disease ravaged every part of him. But it never affected his will. He endured the 1980s chemotherapy and radiation treatments without ever showing me his weakness. If that "Hell on Earth" meant one extra second with his family, he would suffer the entirety with a forced smile. His mind was strong, and his will never cracked through the end. I am sure that seeing him fight is where I developed my insatiable appetite for it. He never gave up, so he never showed me how. My Dad has been my greatest teacher. He led by example whenever I was watching. He taught me with everything he did, and still today, I am actively learning from and guided by his memory. I have much to thank my Dad for.

After Dad died, the YAC group helped our family a lot. Not long after his death, I was invited by our friends, the Goodman family, on what would be my first actual snowboarding trip. We were headed to "Big Sky," Montana, because they were one of the few resorts in the country at the time that allowed and even rented snowboards. There were still no lessons of course. We were on our own to learn to ride them. That thought makes me laugh out loud today.

The 90s were an exciting time for me filled with less regulations and less adult supervision than exists today. I still had my youth, so I bounced back from injuries quickly.

Eric and I rented our first real snowboard equipment. Our boards had steel edges. Wax on the base made them slick to the snow. They were equipped with bindings that held actual snowboard boots firmly to our feet, and the form-fitting boots forced the board to contort under our feet for proper operation. It felt like our first time all over again. We were really snowboarding; we were real snowboarders. At least we looked the part.

As with many first attempts, the first day was discouraging. I think we may have been afraid of the immediate speed. I know I was. It was hard to do anything but immediately go extremely fast.

During the first night, it started to snow, and it kept snowing. It snowed and snowed and snowed. By day 3, it was waist deep, so there was no consequence whatsoever to even what normally would have been a hard fall. It gave us the opportunity to practice a lot without the fear of falling. Eric and I picked up the mechanics straight away, and by the end of our week there, his parents had a hard time getting us off the mountain. Eric and I started by kicking boots up the YAC event hills, and we kept riding together.

Our friendship continues, and not only on the hills. One of our first jobs together was at the local Subway restaurant. It was there, that we made our plan and decided eventually to achieve our Professional Ski and Snowboard Instruction of America certifications at Buck Hill. We became Professional Snowboard Instructors together. Snowboarding fit our personalities, and we fit right in with that crowd. Jake and Tommy were already wearing loud clothes and listening to loud music while they impressed all the loud girls. Eric and I used to go to the Twin Cities to watch the new snowboarding movies that played in the record shops. We also learned to tune our edges on the same hill as Lindsay Vohn. Being a similar age, we heard her name, but I didn't meet her until years later.

Chapter 2

The friendship Eric and I had developed in our youth continued into our adolescence and into adulthood. I'd like to think we have gotten even closer over the years. By the time we got to high school, we had already been riding together for years. I turned 15 towards the end of my freshmen year and was already able to drive on my own, because of a farmer's permit or a bereavement license or something like that. Dad had passed away several years earlier, so I think I qualified for some sort of special circumstance. I was nearly the oldest in my grade, and this, along with my circumstances, allowed me a certain level of freedom.

Eric and I came from similar backgrounds, so we learned the value of hard work as young men. We had more than a few jobs together. We poured concrete, we did landscape work, as well as pulling trap at the horse and hunt club. We also put together sandwiches at the local Subway restaurant. Even at a young age, we knew work meant increased opportunity. We saw that people who worked hard had things and got to do things that others didn't. I can vividly remember the many times our friends rolled through the drive-through at Subway. They loved to play games; as did we. They seemed to enjoy going through all the trouble of ordering a sandwich, but when they pulled up to the window, they would blow a huge lung full of weed smoke directly into the restaurant and then drive away, leaving us to explain. I remember thinking, "What ass holes!" as I quickly attempted to close the window. Awe, ... Those were the days.

I believe that it was at Subway that we decided that the next winter we would give up the daily grind of our many jobs and attempt to achieve our PSIA snowboard instruction certifications. The closest place to slide sideways was, of course, Buck Hill. It took months of driving nearly an hour, both ways, sometimes more, to the hill in order to attend the necessary classes that would eventually lead to our instruction certification.

Eric and I were both successful on our first attempt through the training program. This led to us teaching groups of "knee highs" around 1997 or '98. It was around this same time, that snowboarding was accepted into the Olympics as an official sport for the first time. Eric and I witnessed the sport as it took shape from the early days on, and we were already as big a part of it as we could find a way to be. We chose to make this sport a large part of our lives from early on. We started dragging our knuckles at a young age, and mine never left the ground. Eric and I were great friends all the way through high school, and still today, I can't remember a conflict that we weren't on the same side of.

We were seniors in high school on the 11th of September 2001, "The day the world stopped turning." I remember right where I was. I think we all do. I was a Senior. Our instructors let us out of class, and everyone congregated in and around the locker banks to stare at the live TV feeds, awaiting new views of what they were calling "an attack" on any news stations. As the second plane hit the tower, there were people crying out loud; there were screams of terror and cries of fear. And it was within that second, inside that moment in time, that another piece and perhaps the last piece of my childhood innocence was torn away from me. The kids who had family in NYC could not contain their fear. It burst out of them in uncontrolled gasps. They were at the center of huddled masses. I can only imagine what they felt, but I was horrified. After Dad died, I was the worst kind of scared and helpless imaginable. Was this now what they all felt? Who was responsible for this? I skipped shock and went straight to rage. I could not feel their pain, but my experience made me empathetic. And I could not turn it off. It was familiar to the way that I felt as I watched my dad's body (but never his will) succumb to the disease that took him from his family nearly a decade earlier. But this time was different. The heat inside me smelted a cause, an inherent sense of duty.

I felt, it rose

It gained mass and froze

It darkened, Arise

Broke loose, I cried

Broken, Plunged down

Icy water surround

Engulfed by the deep

Anger will reap

Still leagues away

Tsunami of Rage

Will all too soon prey

When the towers fell in New York in September of 2001, I felt the overwhelming pain of losing my dad all over again. Only this time, it was multiplied by every person lost in New York. I remembered the night that I had to fight to sleep knowing that I would never see my dad again. I imagined how the many kids who lost parents were feeling that night, and the depth of fear that I imagined they were experiencing. And it hurt. It still hurts.

After Dad died, I was introduced to this intense fear and my dependable reaction to it, anger. The anger would follow me for years that turned into decades. When the towers fell, it was already a nearly decade-old source of undefinable, and bottomless strength and resilience. It was with me everywhere, every second of every day. I was a forgotten pressure pot left atop an open flame. My mystic fountain of angry energy required a steady outlet from an early age.

Not long after Dad died, I didn't know what else to do, so one day I just started running. I suppose that could be a metaphor, but I did it literally. After months of training, I completed my first half marathon at the age of 11. I ran next to my cousin the entire way. I could guess that he had his own reasons to run, but it would be a guess. We both found comfort in it.

Running worked for a while, but when the towers fell, something broke loose inside me. For a couple months, I was walking a tight rope every day, barely able to keep my balance. Rage pulsed out of me like blood from the punctured artery of a wounded animal. I felt it gain strength with every beat of my cardinally enraged heart.

Chapter 3

Then as clear as any sign from our creator that I have ever gotten, one Wednesday afternoon, an Army recruiter came to my high school. I think I was easy to spot. All the recruiter did was ask me if he could buy me dinner. This was the answer that I had been waiting for. This is how I would learn to fight back. To protect myself. To finally gain some kind of control. The Army would make me a man; and the world couldn't possibly run over a man the same way it could run over a kid. Or so I thought. The recruiter's job was easy when dealing with a kid like me. When we sat down to eat, he immediately started to tell me why the Army was better than the Marine Corp. He asked me if I was ready to fight, and I didn't need to answer him directly. My answer was written on my face; in my slanted eyes and my gnarled brow line. There was no need for me to respond vocally. He put the contract on the table, and I signed without wasting a second to consider. We finished eating at that local Chinese restaurant, and later that night I told Mom I had joined the Army.

I didn't join our nation's Army, because I was raised to be some huge patriot. My grandfathers both served, but they didn't talk about it to me. I was too young while they were still alive. The truth is that I was raised, like my neighbors, to stand up for what is right, not to tolerate injustice, to believe that giving up was not an option, that nothing good came easy, and never to run from a fight. The recruiter offered me something that I had always wanted but had never really known to look for. He offered me the opportunity to be trained by the best fighting force in the history of mankind.

I was sworn into the United States Army shortly after that, and as soon as I graduated from high school, I left for basic training. I was no true-blue patriot at the start. I was just looking for an adventure. I was fueled by a still undefined and capable rage. I dreamed of seeing the world, of conquering my piece of it, and trying to define peace. The Army sounded to me like a free ticket around the world, and there was almost sure to be at least some level of excitement involved.

Going in, I thought about Basic Training as just the first thing in my way. I was excited to get started, and I had so much fun there. We trained with women at Ft Jackson. I had a girlfriend there named Peres, who helped me enjoy that time in my life. That time flew by, and it was punctuated with achievement. I left there a Squad Leader, already achieving rank and numerous accolades. I left an E2- with high marks for near perfection in both Physical Training and Marksmanship. I graduated top 10% and left with what I thought was a steady grip on what would lie ahead.

I consider myself smart, but I had never thought seriously about college. That was until the Army told me that they would pay for it if I wanted to go. I tested well and joined up as an Army Reserve Engineer. I was told that I would do one weekend of Reserve service a month and two weeks of service a year, becoming an, "Army of one." I did this while attending college like most of my friends did. It gave me a great sense of power, pride, and control. Dangerous ingredients in the mind of an 18-year-old kid? I remained a reservist for all of one month, before I was activated in preparation for my deployment. I did a single drill weekend, where I met the unit that I would never see again. Being the lowest ranking private, I was immediately cross leveled to a deploying unit out of Colorado. The 244th Engineer battalion was located at that time in Boulder, Colorado.

Now, not only was CU Boulder Maxim magazine's #1 party school in the nation at that time, but it was also where my first cousin and good friend had just started school. He immediately joined the ranks of a fraternity called something like "Idios." They would later be kicked off campus for their insane initiation rituals. For example, when they were no longer allowed to drink alcohol they switched to water. Did you know that you can die from drinking too much water? Apparently right before death, one experiences a euphoric state, and the older members of "Idios" talked about being "water drunk" as if it was a point of pride for them. Normally only members could witness this insanity, but considering my situation they let me in on the... fun?

Boulder was perfect for what it was. It wasn't all roses, but it was a great distraction. I quickly lost my taste for the hippy scene, however. They spat on us while in uniform and called us "Baby Killers" while our backs were turned. That was too much.

This Army unit was new to me. A lot of us had been cross-leveled. About half of our new unit was from Wisconsin, the other half being from Colorado. I was the lone Minnesotan. I knew nobody, but I was good at making friends. I was however, struggling to fit in a little and taking more than my ration of shit from a couple of jokers from the Wisconsin group. Their names were Sands and Evans. They each had a few years on me, and they out ranked me, but only just.

Either way, I don't think either of them expected what I'd do next, but they would quickly respect me for it. "Scooter" (Scott Sands) had given me a ration of shit that day, and I warned him that I'd get him back. The whole unit was staying in a hotel. I shared a room with Scooter's adversary from their old unit in Wisconsin. His name was Castro. After Castro put the idea in my head, it went from thought to execution very quickly. I simply approached the front desk and lied about who I was. I told them that my ID was in the room, that is, Scooter and Evan's room. After gaining access to their room, I quickly tossed it. I threw beds against the walls, emptied bags, and put Icy Hot in their boxers...Greatest prank ever, according to me! Evans, however, found the Icy Hot unappealing. Neither was Scooter happy about the toss.

That night, I existed without sleep, on a razor's edge. That was the one time in my life that I breathed into a paper bag. I was constantly afraid that they would gain access to my room, as from the hall they taunted me, "We're going to kill you Deutsch! You little bitch! We know it was you!"

That lasted for what seemed like all night. But then first thing in the morning, Sands approached me, and I saw from a distance the huge smile on his face. He told me directly that my stunt took balls. The laughs that the prank provoked made their way through the ranks, and I'd like to think that they helped to break up the CO and WI clicks and solidify our unit. Plus, I had gained the respect of my peers. As a matter of fact, I'm now the very proud godfather of Scooter's beautiful, and intellectually gifted little dare devil of a daughter. I love you sweetheart.

I also learned not to underestimate the effectiveness of comic relief. I have been lucky to get to know a few world class leaders, and most are quick with a joke. Because, when the situation gets tense, a laugh is a quick way to find common ground. Levity is a powerful tool among people, likely because we all suffer, and enjoy rising above our common suffering by laughing at ourselves. What I'm getting at is that, we're not all that different.

It was around this same time, that I was first introduced to my battle buddy, Crystal Woolen. The story of meeting my "Battle" is one worth telling, because a similar story has saved some 50,000 or more severely injured men and women in recent years. A decision made somewhere up the chain of command...perhaps MG Jim Collins himself gave the order that would place Woolen and me together. We were a perfect fit immediately.

The setting was a formal "dining out." The 244th Engineer battalion was a mix-matched unit composed of many Army Reserve soldiers from around the country. We had a short time during pre-deployment exercises to get to know each other. And so, with this in mind, our CO's (Commanding Officers) threw us a party or what they called a "Dining Out." We wore our Class A uniforms, and we looked good. Then they lined us up like we were in grade school and wrote our blood type on our forehead with permanent marker. Then they told us that only our new "battle buddy" with a matching blood type could wash it off, and that we were to start to go everywhere together. From that point on, I like to think of us as soul mates. Fate put us together, and if I told you the lengths that we have gone to for each other since then, I would be violating her trust, so I won't. I love you Battle.

When a service person is wounded in action, everyone wants to do everything they can to help them. There is no doubt but spending resources on one can mean neglecting another. I heard at one point that no one gets more than 7 pints of blood in the field, and I heard while watching "Trailer Park Boys" that a human body only contains around 10 pints of blood. Now, I imagine that actual numbers vary greatly, and that 10 pints is about as close to the mark as I am after a 12 pack. But my point is still valid for this purpose. With an imaginary 10 pints of blood in our body, I could believe that medical teams are forced to give up after using 7 pints. As one may imagine, that exact number may not be factual, but my point is that there is a standard practice, and that real lives hang in the balance. Unless they have their battle buddy with them that is. Woolen didn't leave my side until they were able to stop the bleeding. I am confident that without her, I would be dead, and so would some other 50,000 severely injured service men and women. There is nothing on earth that I would not do for my Battle if I was able, and I have got a pretty good idea she feels a similar way.

Chapter 4

After months of preparation, the 244th finally boarded a huge 747 commercial airliner. We all wore "full battle rattle." We carried everything we would need on our backs. Everything back home was left in a storage unit. Our gear was heavy. We boarded the flight with our weapons and ammo. We had our kevlars, rucks, duffels, and armor. We carried all our clothing, our DCUs, BDUs, mop gear, knives, MREs, 2 pairs of boots, Runners, PT's and shower gear. We had everything that we would need once we "hit the ground." There was no security checkpoint to board this flight, although it was a surprisingly regular flight, only we had no staff.

When the door opened on the runway in Kuwait, I was probably the tenth person in line to disembark. The heat swallowed us as we stepped onto the jet-way, and we stayed in its fiery belly until we left the country. That time wasn't far off for me. As we continued down the portable jet-way stairs, we were each handed a bottle of water that would last a week in the states. It made a 2-liter soda bottle seem as if it deserved a nipple. But one short hour later, we were all looking for more water. Our DCU's would be crusted and hard with salt deposits before we could find a place to wash them the first time.

After a few weeks there, we had been in Iraq long enough to realize we couldn't tolerate the heat of the day, so we learned to work at night. Most of the time we were incredibly bored. We had a saying in the military, "Hurry up and wait." We were always, "Combat Ready," to sit on our asses. We would gossip about what happened in the showers when nobody was watching. We played endless games of Risk for days on end. We PMCS'd our vehicles. We wrote letters home, and we handed out food and other things we collected from back home to the local children when we went into town. We started to buy local food. and wow! It was maybe the best chicken that I have ever had with these sweet, delicious, little, dark, balls that were not grapes, but not quite raisins yet either; all on a bed of long skinny rice. It was real food, it was really good, and the local people were really grateful for our appreciation. One of us could eat for under a dollar, and we could feed a squad for five dollars.

Any and all money with Saddom Hussein's face on it was worthless overnight. I once gave a haji man one dollar for a piece of money that he told me was worth as much as his house.

While we were allowed to eat local food we ate like kings. We also threw a lot of horseshoes. That was SSG Lawton's favorite thing to do, and it was obvious why. Always leading by example, he showed us a winner with every game he played. Although I remember complaining a lot about being in complete misery, I was among people that I had such a great respect and admiration for. Now, as I look back on those white-hot days and long nights, I admire my friends again for being with me during the most character-building and truly some of the happiest, and believe it or not, most peaceful times in my life to that point.

We entered Iraq from its border with Kuwait in May of 2003. We were an engineering battalion, the first ENBN in country…." ESSAYONS HOOHA." "Essayons," is what one soldier engineer yells to another when in like company. It means "Let us try," and believe it or not, it is meant in a peaceful attempt to prevent war. And "Hooha" is a somewhat similar term among the entire Army. This is a code, a call out, a thank you, an amen to all my combat engineer siblings, and more still to all of my brothers and sisters who have served through the history of our nation's Army. It's a war cry, a call to arms, it signifies that what we have here is worth defending. Still today, "God bless the USA!"

The 244th would be tasked with many odd jobs in the short time that I was with my unit before my injury. We pulled a lot of security at night and transported things on trucks in convoys during the day. We fortified bases and filled sandbags. We collected things from our families back home to give to the children on the streets, who often seemed to be expecting it.

I'll never forget how many stars I could see from our base through a pair of night vision goggles. With so little light pollution, the sky was bright, and the entire Milky Way was vivid. It was obvious why it has been called a river of stars. We counted shooting stars by twos and threes. Although we had a lot of time to do it, watching the stars at night was by no means our specialty. We were after all Engineers…Combat Engineers! HOOHA! Forward progress meant that we traveled up the "highway of death," either occupying Iraqi military compounds or building base camps in the middle of the desert along the way. When we would arrive at an FOB (forward operations base), it would basically be two marines with their backs together and their weapons fixed down-range defending not much more than a spot on a map. I mean, these forward observing marines actually had tanks and entire batteries of artillery. But, when we left, they also had showers and a dining facility, because those were the things that engineering brings to the front lines. They even had a Subway.

The water treatment facility was our first real defense task. It was a security detail. We worked against our will out in the sun all day, under the order of SSG Lawton. We filled sandbags in order to "fortify our fighting positions," fighting positions that did not meet SSG Lawton's personal standard.

After we finished, it didn't take long for us to strip naked and jump in the big water tanks that held the drinking water for the nearby city. It was not even dark, but we were already counting shooting stars and regaling each other with impossible stories from our youth. something that was still playing out for me at only 19 or 20 years of age.

My squad leader could be somewhat of a stick in the mud from time to time. He was a Marine before he joined the Army Reserves. He was very particular about how he liked things done, and it was usually better than the way that I had learned. But I must say, if I needed correction, he was patient. Until he had enough. Then I did push-ups. I have a lot of respect and adoration for all my brothers and sisters in arms. But for reasons that only a jar head (a Marine) can understand, once you join the ranks of the Marines, you are for the rest of your breathing days a Marine. I openly admit a lot of respect and even jealousy over this attribute that only the Marines hold to the highest regard. All branches of service: our Army, our Navy, Airforce, and Marines take the oath, and we all know in our heart of hearts that we would STILL obey that oath to protect our country with our lives even today. However, only the Marines have found this very romantic way to embrace our promise. Also, Marines run on pride. They live for it, and as Marines, they liked to talk about it.

SSG Lawton was no different. But again, I must give credit where credit is due. SSG Lawton's overcompensation, attention to detail, and use of open public scrutiny was effective and would this night save not only my life, but also likely the lives of everyone under his command. We were kept safe by way of his unwavering attention to detail. SSG Mark A. Lawton gave his life first for his family, the one he left back home, Sheri and his two boys, and next, for the family made up of the people he fought next to, his brothers and sisters in arms. Third, he died for every American. He laid down his life for ours, because there are things here worth defending. Finally, because he was able, he felt it was his duty. I can't count the number of times that man saved my life, but I know now with real peace and honesty between our souls, that I didn't get hurt until he was gone. He was a leader, and he led only by example. He was never hypocritical. SSG Lawton always had his family, his troops, you, and the rest of his country in the front of his mind.

We told ourselves that Lawton was just making us work to work, so that we had something to complain about. Misery loves company that way. We would bitch about the little things that he would make us do like filling endless sandbags to fortify our fighting positions, or endlessly cleaning our weapons to rid them of sand. He demanded that we were always "combat ready." He watched closely what each of his soldiers put in their bodies, and he made sure personally that we were always drinking enough water. He checked each of our feet and knew intimately each of our temperaments. For these and many other reasons, I can say with utter confidence that SSG Lawton saved my life that night, and "Private Pussy's" life too. That redundant task of filling sandbags just hours before the attack that day saved our lives, because they weren't only holding sand when the sun rose the next day.

As an Engineer Battalion, we were not very heavily armed. Not compared to other types of units at least. At the water treatment facility, we had a single, "Ma Duce" 50 Cal as well as a single, "MARK 19" automatic grenade launcher. Both were mounted on the roof of the highest building, the only building in the compound. My M249 SAW (squad automatic weapon) was the next biggest weapon except for the Active Army Avenger unit, which was there with us to provide extra fire power. An "Avenger" is a Humvee with a rotating surface to air rocket turret system on the back of it. The Avenger crew referred to units like ours (Reserve Engineers) as POG (Person Other than Grunt) units. We were after all reservists and not full-time soldiers. They thought of us as half civilian. These guys told us earlier that day to try not to get in the way if something went down. However, my training was fresh, so I didn't put too much weight on what these jackasses were vomiting at us. They were wearing the right colors, and that meant that I had a duty and willingness to die saving their lives if need be, just like they would lay down their own in defense of mine. Or so I thought. That is what makes soldiers, sailors, airmen and women, and marines so close once we leave the service, the truth is that once we take that oath, we never take it back. In fact, we long to be surrounded by it the rest of our lives, I imagine this to be similar to the way a Samurai longs for an honorable death. It's what we train for and why we train.

The night of that first attack, we were all together up at the talk, the only Humvee capable of communicating with HQ. If there was a person on the perimeter, they were lonely. The sun had gone down, and it was finally getting almost comfortable; although it had a way of never quite getting there. It was dark, but not late. Something flew over fast, too low to be a plane, but at the same time too high to be offensive. The farmers had no training and terrible aim. We called HQ and asked if there was a test fire or something else planned. We checked to see if there was some, "show of force" that could explain what we saw. Just as headquarters told us that we were likely under attack, the unmistakable racket of small arms fire rang out. It was very likely AK47s again. I could almost recognize that racket by now.

Shoot! Those are tracers! Oh damn!
 Shit! BOOM! A second RPG hit a tree!
Tat, tat, tat! AKs again!

.

We were under attack and taking direct fire. The last explosion was still above our heads, but inside our camp, nonetheless. I felt it somewhere to my left as I ran.

Tat! Tat! Tat! Tat! Tat!

My recently fortified fox hole was 20 feet straight ahead in the direction of the incoming fire.

Tat! Tat! Tat!

Incoming rounds were hitting the trees, buildings, and even dirt in my path.

Tat! Tat! Tat! Tat! Tat!

Every third bullet carried a burning piece of phosphorus called a "tracer" making nighttime combat similar to a scene from Star Wars. The tracers looked like laser beams, stretched out as they traveled across the night sky. Outside the cover of my foxhole, I was a soft target!

Tat! Tat!

Tat! Tat…. Tat! Tat! Tat! Tat! Tat… Tat! Tat…. Tat! Tat!

Training took over when the fight started. I was watching this unfold through the eyes of a Highly Trained American Soldier. His body is strong, and his mind is steady. During training, he was broken down to nothing and built back up with this one purpose in the mind of his designer. Most of you have probably seen this in video games, and that's almost how it felt, except I was very aware that it was not a game. I was aware enough to rely solely on my training.

Tat! Tat!

Within a couple of seconds, I was in my position. My SAW and I were raining down killer hot lead on whatever poor soul mounted the attack. The enemy fire was now drowned out by the temporary reign of my assigned M249 Squad Automatic Weapon. I had no desire to kill anyone, only a deep love for the people that I was with and a complete willingness to do whatever it took to keep them as safe as I could. I was in full soldier mode. I was 10 miles into a 15-mile march wearing 65 pounds of gear. I was on hour six, riding ring mount at 60 mph behind "Ma Dues," while it was 120 degrees outside. The underside of my fingernails were on fire from the never-ending torment of hot wind.

Tat! Tat! Tat!

My training was under control. I didn't want to give away my position, so I used no more than a five-round burst; although my SAW was capable of a nonstop, barrel melting 1000+ rounds a minute.

BOOM! Tat! Tat! Tat! Tat!

Sparks flew as the transformer on the power pole right in front of my fox hole exploded when the 50 caliber Ma Dues entered the fight. Its chest-pulsing authority was felt from my hole and was enough to take the reign of biggest gun straight away from me.

Tat! Tat! Tat! Tat!

It was like a 4th of July fireworks finale gone crazy. It was chaos! With tracers coming in and tracers going out, the entire sky was filled all at once.

Tat! Tat! Tat!

A soldier got thrown into my fox hole by his SGT. It was the private from the Avenger crew.

Tat! Tat! Tat! Tat!

Now, I was busy, but I was not an asshole, so between the fire, I attempted polite conversation.

Tat! Tat!

He was in the fetal position covering his head with his hands.

Tat! Tat! Tat!

I was laughing, prone, only my eyes and barrel visible to the enemy above the sandbags. I'd be a hard target to hit in the dark. Now, I could tell that this guy was a little upset.

Tat! Tat! Tat!

So, I shouted out, between the fire, "Everything is going to be all right man!"

Tat! Tat!

"Keep your head down!"

Tat! Tat! Tat! Tat!

Then he started yelling out something about "going home tomorrow." I was too busy putting hot lead down range to respond in any direct sort of way.

Tat! Tat!

I tried again to console him a little but wondered what was going on. Why wasn't he launching missiles at these fools from his Avenger?

Ta tat! …Tat! Tat!

So, I shouted out between the bursts, "What's going on?"

My SAW was on duty making it nearly impossible to hear.

Tat! Tat! Tat!

"I'm supposed to go home tomorrow!" I heard him shout over the blasts.

Tat! Tat! Tat! Tat! Tat!

He was now gasping as if he would never taste air again.

Tat! Tat! Tat!

Now there was audible sobbing.

Tat! Tat! Tat! Tat! Tat!

This guy was my little sister, and I was giving her a nuggy.

Tat! Tat! Tat! Tat!

Except those are metaphors, and we were in combat and taking direct fire!

Tat! Tat! Tat! Tat! Tat!

We could both feel the percussion of the enemy rounds as they hit the sandbags inches away from us. The same bags that we so begrudgingly packed earlier that day.

Tat! Tat!

"We're going to be fine man!" I reassured him.

Tat! Tat! Tat!

"What's your name?"

Tat! Tat! Tat! Tat! Tat! Tat! Tat! Tat!

"PRIVATE…" he stammered.

Tat! Tat!

"PRIVATE… PUSSY!"

Tat! Tat!

"I want to go home!"

Tat! Tat!

More sobbing...

Tat! Tat Tat!

This continued for a few minutes. At that point, the enemy probably started to catch their breath, because my opened-mouth, deep belly laughs were making it impossible to put rounds on target. Plus, my barrel was so red hot that I could see the rounds traveling through it. It was time to change it out. I decided to wait until the end of the current bandoleer of ammo. I could see, from their tracers, right where they were. We had flares falling over them lighting them up. I couldn't help but pity the people down range.

Just then, a flare fell right in front of me. It landed 50 yards out, right between me and the enemy's position. It effectively lit me up. My position was highly visible, so I hunkered down to wait out the flare. As I pulled my weapon in off the bags that were supporting it, I could again feel the now constant percussion and see the still burning phosphorus from the incoming rounds as they hit the bags that I had just filled. Then, just as quick as it started, it stopped. SSG Lawton called out the cease fire order.

CHAOS! CHAOS! While it lasts.
Am I okay? All over fast!
Where's my Battle? Is she hit?
Ammo, how much left of it?
Are you hurt? Where are you all?
I cannot see you through the fog.
Listen! Now for others' cries.
While I hold back internal sighs.
I wonder how much time has passed.
Reality regained at last…

During the AAR (After-Action Report), I got the scoop. That last RPG that exploded; well, from what "Private Pussy," said, was just feet above his head. I asked him about it later, and I'll use his words as I believe they do most accurately describe his state of mind. "It took every single muscle in my body not to shit my pants man!"

If that was the case, I give the guy credit for making it to my hole under mostly his own power and not smelling of feces.

The truth is that the concussive blast from an RPG that close to a human brain can be just like hitting a reset switch in a lot of respects. For me, some things changed while others didn't. My oldest abilities; the things controlled by the oldest, longest neurons; the ones that nearly inherently take care of things like aggression control, and emotional awareness and control, as well as most of the memories from my youth were shattered like glass. I have no way of knowing they ever existed, so I was lucky. A blast like that can easily leave a man in a catatonic state or in a place where he must learn everything over again; from speech to using the toilet. I have watched close personal friends go from a state where they needed help wiping drool during initial visits to watching them take back control of their family and graduate with advanced degrees. There are thousands of us out there today that appear to be 30, 40, or 50-year-old men and women, who have brains put together still much like children. I like to call it adult onset shaken baby syndrome. I guess I choose to believe that if you succeeded in growing up the first time, before your injury, that you'll only do better the second, or third time. I'm 36 years old now, and I've been a retired vet for well over a decade. Yet, I still look forward to the day when I can say for the first time, while displaying a straight face, "I act like a grown up!"

Chapter 5

More time passed. The days began to string together, making it hard to remember one from the next. I can't say that much about a day's specific events, but I can't totally forget them either. It requires help to determine exactly which memories I've lost since my brain injury, but I imagine the day started out routinely. I would have been excited, because I had heard that there was work to do. There was to be a mission, a convoy, and I was to ride along as rear security. I often volunteered for any mission that I could. I wanted to stay busy, so I could avoid less desirable jobs. Also, I was extremely proud to be our Squad's M249 Squad Automatic Weapon gunner. The SAW replaced the M60. Looking back, I feel honored to have carried that weapon, its 40 pounds of ammo, and its extra barrel. Never mind that I was the smallest guy in the entire platoon, nay company, nay unit.

Back home, I grew up a "country boy"; in the right company, a "hick." So, I started hunting to help provide meat for the dinner table as soon as I was allowed to get my hunter safety certification at the age of ten. I believe I still carry great skill with a duck call. So, I was good with most any weapon I got my hands on. I qualified near perfect on the range in basic training. I did miss a target there at qualification with my M16, but I had an extra round at the end as well. I don't think I saw the first target. I did, however, qualify expert with my SAW; meaning I did not miss a target. With the SAW it almost wasn't fair. I had three rounds to knock over each target. I only needed one, and I could usually squeeze the trigger light enough to only expel two rounds, meaning I would have had extra rounds at the end of that qualification, if I remember correctly. Also, I was ferociously loyal to the people I served with. They became my second family. Even today, there are still things I call on them for that I could never ask of my blood family. Looking back, I would take being a SAW gunner over being a shit burner any day of the week, including Friday, August 29th, 2003.

As our squad's machine gunner, I would often act as rear security. That meant that I would guard our backs, our 6:00 position. Any attacks from the rear would have to get through me first.

Tyler McWilliams (Big Mac) was in the back of the trailing Duce and a half (2.5 ton) truck with me the day that we both earned our Purple Heart Medals. Big Mac was the first face that I saw after the RPG hit us. He was a Hero that day, and I'm sure many since. He did what he was trained to do. He was up near the cab, behind the passenger's seat. The Duce and a half was set up as a troop carrier with mostly benches in the back of it, as well as a lot of gear. I was set up with my weapon resting on the tailgate. I remember the heat of the sun-soaked metal scalding my right leg as I positioned it cornered against both the bed and the tailgate of the truck. Surely this would be a safe barrier from small arms fire.

The day's conversation was not much different from previous ones we had. Most of us, being from Colorado, talked about snow sports quite a bit. Just because it was 120 degrees and blowing outside, didn't mean that we couldn't dream of snow. In fact, that probably provoked our imaginations. Since I had gotten my PSIA certification only a couple of seasons prior, I fit right into the conversations.

Because it was hot and sandy in Iraq in August, we wore ski goggles to shield us from the wind. As we conversed, our eyes were fixed on the horizon, scanning for silhouettes, for muzzle flash, for the, "unknown unknown." We had been warned that there were hostiles in the area, but we didn't know what to expect. They had been telling us this same thing every day.

By the end of 2004, Improvised Explosive Devices or IEDs were the preferred method of disturbing the force. But early in 2003, the enemy had not yet devised those tactics. They did whatever they could to slow us down. They threw rocks at us. They stood in the road, and when we didn't stop, they put their crying babies down in the road in the path of our vehicles. If we stopped for them, suicide bombers jumped on board and blew themselves up, taking our vehicles and our bodies with them, leaving our souls to answer directly for what we were doing. So, we didn't stop.

I am grateful for the part that I played, the part of an often ignorant private. Mine was but to do or die, mine was not to reason why. So, our trucks never stopped. I must thank the person or people who kept our trucks moving, because their dedicated actions surely saved all of our lives many times over.

War is despicable. It is the most despicable thing we do, and yet we choose to do it. I feel remorse for exposing you to that piece of hell. Part of me feels like I went, and I was part of that despicable thing, war, so that you didn't have to. I felt like I was strong enough to bear the burden for the rest. I had a duty to do so, because I felt that I was privileged to live the life that I had been allowed to choose to live. I feel like now that I have told all of you one of my dirtiest secrets, that somehow lessens what I did.

But now, some 15 to 20 years later, I feel it's important to understand what we did over there, and to understand what you, every future and current voting American, asks every soldier, sailor, airman or woman and every marine to do when you elect politicians who have personal interests in the defense industry. Beware the individual who tells you, "It's just business." They are victimizing someone. If we stop building bombs, they will eventually stop exploding. Fights don't end wars. Gandhi asked us to "become the change that we want to see in the world." He also said, "Strength does not come from physical capacity. It comes from an indomitable will." He also stated that "the weak can never forgive. Forgiveness is the attribute of the strong."

      Fire came from our starboard side, if my nautical terms are correct. The racket of small arms (AK47s) fire was familiar by this point, and incoming tracer rounds are hard to miss. I saw where they were coming from right away. Their muzzle flash was obvious. They didn't stand a chance. I let loose on whoever was firing at us. Anonymous hot lead flew, zapped down range with the excitement of tracers attached to every third round, and with the aid of the tracers, I could see my rounds hitting the sand to the left of my intended target. I realized immediately why. Our truck had picked up speed as soon as the fire fight started. As soon as I saw my rounds fall, I realized and attempted to compensate. I saw my rounds hitting the dirt, not what I wanted. So I walked my rounds onto my intended target. I had been trained not to use more than a 3-5 round burst of fire, so as not to give away my position. However, there was no time for a burst. My rounds were not hitting what I needed them to, so I held down the medicine and let hell fire ring until I was putting hot lead on what threat that I decided to be the most dangerous. I had no rigid ill intent against the poor souls that were trying to kill us, and as far as I know, they none against us. I knew they didn't have a choice. But that was my position, and I was well trained about what to do. Or so I thought. Perhaps it was the fact that I didn't let up on the trigger that drew their attention. A normal 3-5 round burst would make sure that the enemy couldn't easily differentiate my SAW from any other M16. My constant muzzle flash, however; likely gave away my position. I was the next biggest threat to our enemy in that fight. Looking back, if that grenade hitting me meant it didn't hit Big Mac or Battle, then I'm glad, and I would do it all again. I recall seeing a ball of light on fast approach. I had no time to react…...

I'm Hit

I could not hear; I could not smell.

My senses they all went to hell.

I was here now, still was I there, how?

No sound at all from anywhere now.

Where's my weapon? Oh no! oh no!

But still I cannot see my foe.

My vision had yet to return,

Still could not hear,

Felt a slight burn.

I'm sitting in a puddle now,

My mind, it's all a fuddle, how?

My right leg trapped,

Still I can't see.

Why am I wet?

Did I lose my pee?

My vision comes back,

Almost wish it didn't.

What's left of my leg is all torn to ribbons.

The puddle is blood, my blood,

Oh shit.

I cry out to my friend,

"Big Mac, I'm hit!"

His reaction was quick! Stop bleeding, do triage.

My mind, still a blur,

No shape, but a mirage.

My first surprise,

Vision sorted out,

No fear of demise,

This will hurt no doubt.

I simply now wondered not if,

but how,

Will I snowboard without?

By the time our vehicle stopped, I had been sitting in that puddle of blood for what felt like too long. The puddle was large, and I was getting cold. Mr. Ryan Anderson was our combat medic. He did everything that he was trained to do with a steel-eyed reserve, appearing to never be shaken. Anderson saved my life under the worst conditions imaginable. Still a hero, today he fights fires in Littleton, Colorado.

The tourniquet that he tied hurt like the most intense pain that I imagine our bodies are capable of experiencing. I don't feel like words can accurately portray what I was feeling. I was on FIRE!!! Every cell in my body was on fire, and I could feel all of them; I was in shock. He had to turn the tourniquet tighter to stop the bleeding. He turned it tighter and tighter as I swung and punched and spit and cussed and fought. I never quit fighting. It's not in me to quit. I never saw anyone do it growing up, so I didn't know it was an option. And shoot, I guess I still don't.

We could not clear an LZ (landing zone) for a chopper, so we took the hospital Humvees to the nearest CASH Casualty Area Support Hospital. Imagine a MASH hospital tent. It was a staggering 45 minutes or so away. As they were moving me, they kept asking me questions that pissed me off. My angry energy was now the only thing keeping me alive. Good thing I never found the end of it. The medics were trying to keep me angry, and it wasn't hard. It all came out of me! I was eternal anger, I was pure emotion, only my stubborn will kept me alive.

"What's your name soldier?"

"Name, rank, and number?"

"What day is it?"

"Stay with us DEUTSCH!"

"Keep fighting Deutsch!"

"You're going to make it Deutsch. You're a fighter DEUTSCH!"

I think the only response they got was, "Screw you! Where's my weapon?"

The ride to the CASH hospital haunted my dreams for years; until I took control of the memory by writing the account of it and exposing perspective and this fact: although SSG Lawton had already passed, his last move on earth still inspired me to live.

I saw his hand when I closed my eyes at night for many years. Before I realized what he had done for me, the memory continued to frighten me. Now I hold it as close as any I have of the man. I recall the ride in the Humvee. I was on the lower bunk, but there was a bunk above me as well, and there was someone on that bunk. However, when I asked who it was, the medics told me nothing. I got the feeling that whoever it was had to have been KIA, because they were not paying them any attention. Then we hit a bump, and SSG Lawton's arm fell from the bunk above me. His hand hung next to my face for only a second, before they moved it, but I only needed a split second to recognize his wedding band. I recognized familiar calluses on his hand, and I knew that it was my squad leader, Staff Sergeant Mark A. Lawton. He had set the ultimate example. He died as he lived, a HERO. He was Killed in Action, defending freedom the world over. He was leading by example that day, in the lead vehicle when we started to take fire. I believe his death was caused by a head wound from an AK47.

No matter what they said, I knew, so I kept asking "Who's hurt, where are they? Where is my weapon?"

I couldn't turn off the pain. It was agonizing, and I was going fuzzy. But the thought that Lawton had been taken reintroduced me to my old faithful. My mystic fountain of angry energy came back all at once like a shot of adrenaline. It gave me what I needed to survive.

If my dad hadn't been sick in my youth, I would have died. I would not have known fighting that hard was an option. My dad's death gave me the angry passion to survive, and SSG Lawton's death reintroduced me to it. Without either I would have simply gone into the light. Believe it or not that has been an option for me more than once.

Getting out of the Humvee was tough. They loaded me onto a stretcher with wheels under it. I could feel every bump on the way into the tent. I was in rough shape. However, I was young, and I had not yet had any medication, so my mind was already becoming focused on what would be most important to any young man who has just sustained major damage to the lower half of his body.

You know, I think the medics appreciate a patient who fights. I know she did. I forget her name, but she was a Major, and I'll bet that she remembers me. As they were wheeling me into this tent, I remember asking the Major for a blanket, because I was cold. She smiled at me with the face of an angel and told me that I'd be alright.

"Who's hurt mama… Where are they?" I begged her frantically. I was not giving up.

"My boys, Mama, how are my boys?"

She told me that the rest of my unit was okay and that no one else was hurt. At this point, I was not interested in her lies, and that's not what I meant that time anyhow.

"Mama, my boys!?!"

Now she was just ignoring me, and that I could not abide. I needed an answer, and I was afraid to look. So, I grabbed her hand and shoved it down my pants.

Then, I looked her right in her very surprised eyes and repeated myself, "Mama, how are my boys?"

She chuckled for half a second, offered a brief encounter with my man parts, and then smiled as if she knew then that all was going to be okay. She told me that I was going to be just fine. I think that's about when the drugs hit me.

My *Darling, Exceptional girl. Every time I see you my heart lights up like a fire work on a dark night. I love you so much more. Darling, Never forget what I'm about to tell you. You, Can Not Fail Before YOU Decide To Give Up. You Can Do Anything. And if you never forget about the Golden Rule, no one will stop you.*

Chapter 6

"The only thing to fear is fear itself."

I did not fear death on Friday, August 29th of 2003. I didn't fear death in 2007, when I woke up after 10 days in a coma following my motorcycle wreck. That was the most peaceful time in my life, hands down; and I remember it fondly today. I didn't fear death in 2010 on East Colfax; when I was stabbed defending my would-be wife from a mugging in Denver. And I don't fear death today. I trust that if you are proud of the life you are living and have lived, then you have no reason to ever fear anything at all really. Having been very close to death no less than three times, I can tell you with confidence that death is a release. It is scary, because no one has ever told us what will happen, although many have tried. Also, I can tell you that the fear subsides as soon as you quit fighting. Death is a sure escape from life; all of life amounting to some level of pain.

So, I think Roosevelt was close when he spoke about fear. The idea of it makes us do irrational things, and that's what he wanted to pull his nation out of. But I see fear a little differently than he did. I see real fear most often used as a weapon. I see men (mankind) who assume they have power use fear as a weapon. I dare to call it the most successful weapon in history. So perhaps Roosevelt may have missed a layer. Or perhaps he was wielding it. I just assert that blaming fear, for itself assumes that the fear men use for control is somehow responsible for itself. And that asserts that a weapon in and of itself can be responsible. That is not logical as no inert object in the history of existence has ever had control over anything. No bomb, no gun, no arrow, no rock or sharpened stick has ever killed anything. People and more often societies, build weapons to induce fear in other people, so that they can manipulate the resources of said people. We, Americans, do this under the guise of "protection" and "defense," but the story is as old as agriculture itself. We have been doing this as long as societies have been able to produce more than they need to survive. Most of the time it takes people to kill people. In the United States of America, guns are a protected right. That idea was meant to protect us from fear and the inevitable persecution of people who assume they have power.

Absolute power corrupts absolutely! I'd like to simplify that in our society. Today I believe that, All Power is corruptible. That means we will need our guns. Anyone who has read a history book may feel compelled to agree; as disarming the general population has been a sure sign of the end of many entire civilizations throughout history. I am not so arrogant that I think we have changed. Although I do think us capable.

When I am faced with fear, I fight. I turn on survival mode. Our world's fighting forces have had eons of experience weeding out the soldiers that respond unfavorably in the face of fear. To me fear is nothing but a weapon, a threat. And although it is perhaps the greatest weapon in history, like any weapon, it is powerless without a living force to wield it.

For my daughter's 8th birthday, she asked me for a unicorn that pooped world peace. Cheers Darling! I am so proud of you.

Chapter 7

I have no idea how long I stayed at the CASH. It could have been hours; it could have been days…but somebody did manage to bring most, if not my entire platoon, through to see me before I left. I am so grateful for that.

Although I don't remember much of it, I do remember feeling like I had my own job to do after they had gone. I said goodbye for now to my battle buddy, Woolen, and we swore we would see each other again. Scott Sands gave me a level of comfort there. I was allowed a sense of closure. I got to tell Sands that I knew he wouldn't be used to holding anything as big as my SAW, but that I thought he would manage it best. I don't remember if our meeting happened during the day or at night, for they were one and the same during the first weeks after my injury.

From there, I did a quick stop in Kuwait, because I think there was a central hospital there, although I don't remember much of it. I really wasn't back in my own head until I arrived at the hospital in Landstuhl, Germany. While I was there, my good friend, Sgt. Soper, stayed with me until we journeyed all the way back to the states. He chaperoned me. I'm guessing my command knew I might give the nursing staff a hard time. Today, I think of him as more of a "wing man." The guy stood up for me like I was his cub. I remember little from that time. There was a lot of drug use on my part. I was not interested in feeling anything. I vaguely remember a nurse expressing her concern that I was "pressing the button too much." Soper quickly made sure her opinion didn't spread. Soper and I got to meet Lieutenant Dan, from the movie, "Forest Gump", played by Gary Sinees, while we were in Germany.

After about a week, I was transported to Washington DC to do a large part of my recovery at WRAMC (Walter Reed Army Medical Center). During the plane ride back to the states, a nurse put a "hug me" sign on my chest, so everyone who walked by stopped and gave me a hug.

I remember waking up to them scrubbing wounds and sewing me back together several times.   For the first few weeks after the explosion, time had no day or night. There was little difference between conscious and unconsciousness. The mid-night vacuum dressing changes were important to stay clean, and their schedule was concrete. No matter the time of day, no matter the circumstances, no matter my willingness at times… my bandages were changed on time from day one.

I can't remember ever being disappointed in my care. Although I often fought them as I fight everything, every step of the way. The VA staff remained fearless. If I got to one of them, as I could do if I were angry, there was a new face to take over. I was never alone, and if I had a concern, it immediately became the concern of the staff, without exception.

I am glad that I experienced every second of the pain that came with the loss of my leg, because the thing about physical pain is that we can't really remember it. I know that it hurt intensely, but the nerves only fire when they are on fire. We are not built to recall physical pain. In a way, we're not capable of remembering it. It is no secret that we all fear pain, because we are aware that it will hurt. Because of that, we want to avoid it.

But ask any mother how bad the pain of childbirth was, and most will say the same thing. It was the worst pain in their life. Yet I'd argue that a good portion of them try for another child. My Grandma Weiers raised 14 kids and tried 16 times. Being surrounded by such strong people, I did not know weakness in my youth. You may have never had your mouth wired shut or experienced anything close to the agony of an appendicitis or a bowel obstruction. Although I experienced excruciating pain from these, I have forgotten that pain.

Chapter 8

I remember the day, and even the second, that they were able to make the pain go away once I got to Walter Reed. It didn't last forever, but it was effective while it lasted. I was lying on a table and someone had a large

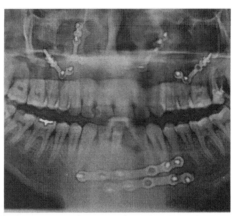

needle pushed some length into my lower back. He was struggling to find the right spot. I was struggling to stay conscious. Then he hit it. He had managed to insert what I imagine was an epidural, and it shut off the pain to the lower half of my body. Just like a light switch, it all turned off at once.

I remember thinking nearly immediately, "Wow, I could almost sleep.... what the shit is going on?"

Just then, a doctor said calmly, almost as if he was no longer afraid to approach me. "Keith, it's nice to meet you, my name is Doctor… you are at Walter Reed Medical Center in Washington, back in the states. Welcome Home! You made it"

I still woke up begging for my weapon back and asking for the location of my battle buddy, Woolen, for what could have been weeks.

Chapter 9

Every service member, who has seen combat, has come face to face with the fear of death. We never feel more alive than we do when we are surrounded by and immersed in the fear of death. Typically, people walk away from experiences where they could come into close contact with death. However, all service members and even some civilians aim for this, because of the perspective it allows. We commonly call these people "Adrenaline junkies."

Service members returning from combat are tuned similarly to these brave souls. I met some of these people when I learned to kayak a few years after the loss of my leg. Sometimes these civilians call on military vernacular to get our attention. Amongst the cadre of Joe Mornini's "Team River Runner," kayaking was referred to as, "White Water Combat." Like in

military combat, kayaking continuously slaps you in the face with the fear of death. Also, similarly, it requires a well-trained, "platoon" of people to achieve an acceptable level of safety or even just to collect "river spoils." Either way, "Booty beers" are common. This is when a kayaker is required to consume a beer. However, the beer must be consumed out of the boot worn by the person who saved their butt on the river that day.

Imagine yourself securely strapped into your new kayak. You are headed for a confluence. You are fully aware of this, because of the commanding walls of the canyon, and the continual echoing of the roaring and tumbling water only grows louder. You have a hard time hearing your friends over the sound of the turbulent river long before you see the wall of fast moving, high volume, completely unavoidable, tumbling rapids.

In that moment, you are hurled back into the fight, and you are alive, but only just. Because deep within that second, you become acutely aware that life could be stripped from you before the next tick of the atomic clock. Time all but stops. You lose your ability to breathe as you are hurdled under the water. Which way is up is suggested only because you are securely strapped into a buoyant boat. Only now, up is under your butt. One can come to enjoy this loss of control if one is willing to experience it enough times to become comfortable. You do it again and again until it no longer scares you; it awares you. That's how you build reactions into instincts.

Facing death, forces to the surface all the jubilance life can/is capable of containing. You are reconnected to the whole, if only for the time you are lost to this world, and there you are allowed to glimpse the next, or to connect with the past. You are aware of everything. I would argue that you don't even know you are living until you have just about died. It's a shame that most people will only ever have this figured out for a couple fleeting seconds before they die. This idea, this knowledge, this awareness has brought me a kind of freedom that's hard to describe in terms bound to this world. Add to that the feeling that you just fearlessly wrestled Mother Nature herself and lived to tell the story. Another similarity between kayaking and actual combat is the feeling of relief that takes over upon exiting the rapids safely. I would say that is very similar to the feeling a service member feels as they return to their base after completing a convoy through enemy territory.

I was so extremely lucky to survive my injury. Many well- trained people had to do exactly the right thing in exactly the right order under very extreme circumstances for me to "hop" away from my injuries, and I am so very grateful to each of them. Also, I am sincerely sorry for being such a DICK. I was not processing my grief past anger.

I would meet more than a few celebs over the next few months and years. Every one of them, first apologized for sending me over there, and then graciously thanked me for my service. One day after my mother had arrived to stay with me, a nurse walked in and told us that Mel Gibson was on the ward, and that he wanted to meet us. I imagine I immediately scoffed; I would not have found that worth getting out of bed for. Sorry Mel, it's not that I am not a fan. I grew up watching you. I just wasn't feeling well. But Judy Deutsch had another idea. Either she really wanted to get me up and moving, or she really wanted to meet Mr. Gibson. I'm sure that both are true. I'd encourage you to ask her about it. I'll let you think whatever you like. Either way, it was clear that I had no choice.

From the time I was hit and throughout the 90 or so days of my physical recovery, I was surrounded by the greatest amount of love that I have ever experienced. The resources spent on my recovery would be hard to account for in monetary terms. I truly feel there was no expense spared, and even if you added up every dollar, that would not hold a candle to the amount of love that I felt. I healed quickly because of the love and support that I had surrounding me.

Chapter 10

He told me first thing to call him Jim, taking rank out of the equation. Jim was another great leader that has remained in my life. Jim was the 2 Star Major General that deployed over 4,000 soldiers from his 96 RRC Regional Readiness Command, including my unit, the 244th Engineer Battalion. He

was the one who delivered the news of my injury personally to my mom.

When I met Major General Jim, I had been known at Walter Reed on the amputee ward as a "tough nut to crack." I remember the Army Chief of Staff, General Shinseky, strolled into my room one day for what I felt was a photo-op. I wish I had a second chance at the conversation. I later learned that he is also missing part of his leg, and that he has also completed marathons as an injured man. It would have been great to make that connection, however, I was still too angry to listen to anyone, so I was not very diplomatic. I wish I could apologize to him directly for my chosen words, but I can't. Sorry Sir. Your story has given me motivation. My words were effective in getting him out of the room. I don't think he got his picture with me. But I know I wish he had. I am lucky I didn't get a court martial.

So, when MG. James Collins walked in, I attempted the same. However, he was not one lick afraid of me. He took one look at me, and it was apparent that he admired the fire in me, so he quickly put me at ease.

He said, "Keith, I'm the highest-ranking person in this hospital right now, and you can't make me leave. I took a few days off to come see you, because you were the first of my 4,000 soldiers deployed to get injured, and I plan to spend the time with you."

He then surprised me by asking what I planned to do with the 1969 Mach 1 Mustang that my father had left in the barn on my mom's farm. Obviously, he had done his homework before he came to meet me. Then Jim took out a photo album of the cars that he had been rebuilding in his spare time. He knew about all the cars that Dad had spent his life collecting, and for that week, I enjoyed the idea that I would have the chance that my dad never got, to rebuild those old steeds to their once great glory.

Dad had an affinity for Love Era muscle cars. He had at least one from each of the big three. I don't remember a Dodge. Dad was a blue oval man through and through. The Ford Mustangs were his pride. When he looked at what he had collected, he did not see the shabby piles of rust that the hard Minnesota winters provoke. In his mind's eye, they were still shiny and new. He had Mom sitting shot gun, and they were rocking out to the Beach Boys. I could see the reflection of these once proud steeds in his eyes.

I will omit some of his collection, not because I want to, but because I was young, and I don't remember all of them. All late 60s cars, they represent love and passion; they represent unbridled freedom and opportunity. They represent a chance at the old American Dream, before it got complicated, a chance at happiness, and that's how they made Dad feel. I guess my devotion to these old things is not hard to explain. Seeing them and smelling them run again makes me feel like I'm three years old and in my Dad's arms again.

What I remember as his favorites were an old Goat (GTO). He always used the word "Rocket" when he talked about it. He had a Chevy, Nova. He had some more obscure projects as well. It will fall to me to rebuild the 1918 Brisco. But the 1969 Mach 1 Mustang was his pride, and seeing us in it, his joy. That car belongs to my big brother, Nick, and I Dream of us putting it together one day.   Dad loved to talk about the Mach One. But there was also a car that he didn't really talk about. I found it buried under a 30-year pile of junk last summer and got it running with little effort. It smelled great. I was home for a family reunion on Mom's farm. After I unburied it, I pushed the white Mustang out of the barn where it had sat for 20 years. It was last registered in 1991, it had a sheriff sticker in the wind screen, the back window was busted out and the stereo was missing. To me, the story was all but obvious.

Since I was at a family reunion, so I asked my aunt about the car. Then I fell head over heels in love as hard as I ever have with an automobile. Aunt Pat said, "Oh you know your Dad, he couldn't say no to anyone." She continued to tell me that Dad had done some lady a favor. After her father died, he left a motorcycle that didn't run in his estate. It wasn't worth anything in that condition so she asked Dad if he could fix it. Dad operated Ron's Cycle Shop on the family farm when he was not plowing the fields. He agreed to fix it, but he said he would not do it for free. He asked her if she had anything on that big farm her dad had left her that she might want to trade.

To that she replied something like "Well, the sheriffs just dropped off an old car, it has a pony in the grill." That's all it took.

"I'll take it," Dad replied. It took little work to get it running. I even found the title. It turns out that Dad stumbled onto a C-code 1964.5

Mustang with a factory two barrel 289.

The story of the Ford Mustang is not a usual one. Most cars are released at the Detroit auto show, or at least they were back then. I'm not sure how Detroit is doing now, but the Mustang was released mid-way through the year in 1964 at the New York auto show. Now, people claim that all the records were lost as to how many of these cars were produced. But a few things are clear. Any 64.5 Mustang is harder to find than even Nick's Elanor, 69 Mach

One. Beyond that most 64 Mustangs were produced with a Ford 300 straight 6 engine. (Maybe the greatest straight six ever built.) The car Dad left was a thoroughbred C- Code car. This meant that it came with the two-barrel 289 V-8 engine package. In fact, the only harder to find, more rare Mustang to ever be produced was the 1964.5, A-Code Car. For a couple hundred bucks a prospective buyer could request that their new Ford Mustang come equipped with a four barrel 289 V-8, giving them extra horse power, and a little edge over everything else on the road.

   Jim told me that my dad was obviously a smart man as there weren't many of those made. He said the only rarer Mustang that existed was the 64.5 GT with the factory equipped 4 barrel, the A-Code 64.5. He informed me that in the right condition, that car was nearly priceless. Needless to say, the man got my attention from the get-go, and he would have it for the rest of my life. I can't say it enough. With all of my heart, Thank you, Sir.

Chapter 11

No one person supported me more than my Mom, Judy Deutsch. Here is my favorite picture of Mom and me as we finished our first running race together in 2017.

It was her first half marathon and my second. We didn't win. But I didn't see two bigger winners all day. Mom always inspires me to excel, because she isn't one to make excuses.

By the time I got back to the states, back to Walter Reed, I had already completed a good portion of my hospital stay. Not long after I got there, I called home. I had a phone and a television connected to my hospital bed. One night, I told mom that I hurt, and that I wished she could hold my hand, then I went to sleep. I woke up the next day to Mom holding my hand, and she didn't leave my side. I later learned that nearly my entire command staff worked tirelessly to make that happen. With what I can only describe as the instinct of a lioness, I watched Mom redefine courage as she stood up to the most powerful man in the world on my behalf.

I met many people who I felt wanted their picture taken with those of us who were most severely injured. It was part of the game. President George W. Bush even pinned a medal to my chest.

Everyone on the ward knew he was coming that day. The Secret Service swept the entire hospital before he got there. While the staff was busy preparing for him, all the patients on the ward were put into a small room, where we were to meet the Presedent many hours later. While we were in that room waiting, we were perhaps a trifle neglected. That is from my narrow perspective, mind you. My colostomy bag had needed changing for hours when the President finally arrived.

There were colored marks on the floor where he would stand. They attempted to plan every detail. But good-old George W. went off script when he got to my mom. I was the last one in line. My missing leg seemed a small loss when compared to the other injuries in the room. When the President finally got to me, I was doing my best to hold back my tears, and I was afraid my colostomy bag was going to explode all over the most powerful man in the world, my commander and chief. There had not been a nurse in the room for what felt like a few hours. At this point, I had not even learned to change it myself. In fact, I don't think I was ever asked to do it while I stayed with the VA. I was also at a level of increased pain; and probably experiencing opioid withdrawals at this point, as well. After he said what he had to say to me, the President of the United States of America approached Mom. I would wager the man was nervous to stand in front of the mother of a child, a 20-year-old young man that he had condemned to this fate. I overheard Mr. Bush express true concern as he asked my mom if I was going to be okay, and here's the funny part. With all the gumption of a woman standing up for and worried about her son, Mom looked G W straight in the eyes and asked him if he wanted to know the truth.

Then the President broke ranks. He extended his right arm and placed his hand on Mom's shoulder, as he whispered something like, "Of course I do, Judy. You can tell me anything."

Mom brushed a tear from her eye and went on to explain to him that everyone in the room needed care nearly constantly. An hour without it, meant a certain level of increased pain and discomfort. Then, I watched the look on his face change and a clear sense of compassion wash over him as she continued to tell him that we had been in that small room for what was now more than a few hours. The President's eyes widened, and his mouth fell open for a second as he realized his unwitting fault in this.

George W. Bush is known not to waste words. His reply made me chuckle as I overheard him say, "Judy, that's when you tell me to just get the **** out of the room."

Then he turned toward the door, and he continued to break ranks as he marched into the hall and used all his voice to shout, "HEY, these guys need care in here!"

As if they were all waiting in line, each of our personal nurses entered the room with haste and pain meds already in hand. You may not like the man politically, and I won't go there, because I volunteered to die at his command, but I am confident that if you ever met him, he might win your favor. My money is still on GW, and I'd be interested to see how he is progressing with painting the pictures of the injured. I thought that a noble cause.

George W. was the biggest name I would encounter while on the ward, but I do not feel that he was the most important, not to my recovery anyway. Later that week, I met the man who would give me hope and impact my life greatly! His name is Kirk Bauer. He would offer me my snowboard back. Kirk walked into my room wearing shorts, making his prosthetic knee obvious to me. He was already wearing the leg that I would soon request. This meant that he was a prior serviceman, and wouldn't you know it? He had a beautiful woman named Tracy with him.

Kirk possessed many gifts of character, and I'll do my best to describe a few of those qualities that ranked him higher in influence than the President in my eyes, but I entirely expect to fall far short. Kirk never made a single promise. In fact, Kirk didn't have to speak much at all. Kirk is a gifted listener, and he is truly one of the greatest motivators of our time. He made what he considered small offers that first time we met. He told me about his event, Disabled Sports USA's "Ski Spectacular", where he would let me try to snowboard if that's what I wanted to do. Beyond that, Kirk did his homework before he ever entered my room that first time. He already knew things about me, things that he felt were going to be important to me and my recovery. In addition, Kirk never lied to me, but at the same time, I had trouble believing what I saw and what he told me. Kirk had everything in common with every good leader that I have ever had the pleasure or duty to follow. He led by example, never expecting me to do anything that he would not first show me how to do. The greatest example that I can think of is getting back on snow. Not only had Kirk already learned to ski after losing his leg, but he told me this story years later, when I interviewed him for this project.

Kirk was leading his squad on a patrol through Vietnam in the late 60s. As a lieutenant, it was not his job to lead patrols, because that is what privates were for. He knew that the least trained men on the battlefield were the most expendable. I understood that all too well, as I was a private carrying an M249 when I was injured. But Kirk didn't take that lightly. He had new soldiers with him that day in Vietnam, so he felt it was his job to lead the way, and that is what he did. In the middle of the patrol, one of his more experienced men called, "Stop!"

The man under his command shouted, "Sir, I don't like this."

And then he fired a grenade a few yards out front of them. The grenadier hit his mark never able to see anything but suspicion. Then Kirk himself approached the now injured Vietnamese man and captured him as a POW. Kirk led by example and listened to his men. This is how a good leader gains the respect of the people under his command.

I had had a drill sergeant during my basic training that led in this same manner. He embodied the true definition of being a good leader! This man was built like GI Joe. He kept himself looking that way every time that he was visible to us, with not one single exception. But that is not what I remember most about him. This guy had everyone in my basic training class convinced that he slept standing up in the wall locker in his office.

Every night as he called, "Lights out!", he would call one of us into his office, the only visible exit from which was the door that led to where we all slept. We pulled shifts to stay up and watch for this guy to leave, but we never caught him. After we entered his office, he would step into his wall locker and stand at attention, apparently until he woke the next morning. After he stepped in, he would order whoever he called into his office to place a lock on the locker door. For the first couple of nights and perhaps weeks, we all knew, thought, or assumed that as soon as we put him in there, he would escape by some unknown exit and return home. I am now sure that, that is what happened, but not one of us was ever able to prove it. After months of letting him out of a sealed wall locker in the morning, it became impossible for even the surest of us to deny. I would have followed that man into hell. Ha, maybe I did.

As a young lieutenant, Kirk later lost his leg to a land mine. It sounds like he was in the lead again to me, although I didn't ask. After his injury, he too was pulled away from the fight. Kirk already knew what thoughts were rolling around in my head, before I had a chance to sort them out for myself. I was thinking about my old life. I was thinking about the sports that I used to love to play, and how I was going to live the rest of my life productively in any kind of familiar way. What kind of girl would want a guy with one leg? And how was I going to keep going after such a large part of me had been taken away?

Before the Army, I had been a champion Minnesota wrestler and already a professional snowboard instructor. I had all but lost hope of any kind of a familiar life until I met Kirk; he changed all that immediately. When he walked in, he had already answered every hard question that I would want to ask him without ever opening his mouth, and that is Kirk's greatest gift. Kirk speaks louder with his actions than anyone I have ever known. He was right up there with Dad and my GI Joe Drill Sgt.

It is impossible to deny what we see right in front of us, and although I've offered this story about his injury now, in order to give credence to my point, Kirk did not tell me this story until we talked years later about this book. Kirk led by example throughout my recovery. He talked briefly about his injury, when I asked directly, but mostly he just listened to me. Nearly immediately, the subject of the conversation turned to winter sports.

Kirk was a skier after his injury. He called his sport "three tracking." Basically, it was skiing on one leg with outriggers attached to

poles held in each hand.

Now, I met Kirk in mid-September, and he told me then that I was invited to his event, "Ski Spectacular", as soon as I was able to attend. He said it might be tough to achieve this year, being held already on December 2nd, but he gave me a goal. Kirk told me that when I was ready and healed enough, I was invited to Breckenridge to learn to ski.

I stopped him right there and said," Sorry sir, but I gave up skiing years ago. I'm a PSIA certified snowboard instructor."

He told me later that that terrified him, but in his reply, he was honest, "I'm not sure I know anyone doing that, Keith."

I was already ecstatic and never afraid to fail, so I butted in, "Well sir, my name is Keith Deutsch, now you do!"

That is the moment I made up my mind that I would keep snowboarding. I had no idea how hard it would be. I had no idea if it was possible. But I saw that people were going to help me, and that gave me all the confidence I needed, and that was enough for Kirk. He then told me that if I was ready by the beginning of December, that I was invited to come to Ski Spec. Now that was an ambitious goal, however, nobody ever put the word "can't" in my head. Today I still don't use that word when talking to my daughter. I don't feel that word is appropriate for children.

Chapter 12

My oldest sister, Jessica, was to be married in mid-October. Since Dad had already died a decade earlier, she asked me to walk her down the aisle alongside my big brother, Nick, if I was able. I remember feeling very grateful for being able to attend. But also, it was still bittersweet being pulled away from my unit. The wedding was an even more ambitious goal than Ski Spec, because her wedding was less than a month away, and I was still weeks away from even being fitted for my first prosthetic leg. Also, I was still living in DC. I would have to remain as clean as possible; navigating infection was an every minute affair. I kept it at the front of my mind. This goal was one that I am convinced was only accomplished through prayer, positive will, grit, and God given stubbornness. The first step was to get transferred closer to home. That way a day trip for the wedding could be a reality.

Then one day, Senator Mark Dayton wanted to say thanks. My ever-brave mom saw an opportunity. She told him how much easier it would be if I could be transferred to the Minnesota VA for the rest of my care. We were on a flight the next day. That was the only time in my life to that point that I got to fly first class. The pilot acknowledged my mother and I were on the flight, and Mom didn't stop saying, "You're welcome," for the entirety of the flight. She protected me from having to answer people directly and allowed me to rest.

By the time I got to Minnesota, however, I had developed a new problem. Some shrapnel had pierced my belly area. It tore through my intestine making it impossible to process food in any kind of familiar way. Therefore, eating all of the chocolate that people were sending me had negative effects. They opened me up, they took all of my intestines out, sewed up all the holes, shoved them all back inside, and stitched me back together.

A week later, I was to attempt putting food in my mouth for the first time in a while, and I guess I made a mistake. They allowed me to head down to the DFAC (dining facility) unattended. I think they may have mentioned to stay away from popcorn as it could cause a block. So, what did I do? I did what I think any 20-year-old would have done when he hadn't eaten anything in a few weeks. I filled my tray with everything that I would like, and I started by taking small bites of each thing to see if it hurt. It didn't, so I kept going. I had jalapenos on a burrito. I had spaghetti and a wonderful cheesecake. Coffee was on the menu, soda, steak, everything that I had been craving for months now. I don't even remember being asked to pay for it. Needless to say, I may have gone a little overboard.

The following bowel obstruction lasted ten days and was the closest I came to death throughout this whole ordeal. By far the worst part was that pain. It felt like someone was twisting a knife in my belly for ten days. Pain meds tend to slow down the digestive system. So, for those ten days, I endured without narcotics. The pain associated with my leg was small compared to the agony of the bowel obstruction, however, it was in no way easier because of it. I think I understand why they just shoot horses. Trust me, when I say that I am surprised that I survived. I taunted death and called on the reaper loudly to come take me. But what I never stopped doing was fighting. I was never shown how to quit fighting, and so that was never an option.

Then one day, a big burly guy wearing nurses' scrubs entered my room. I could have sworn at the time that he was the angel of death. He was a nurse, but all my other nurses were cute young women. I enjoyed flirting with them. So, I was caught off guard when this guy walked in. I knew something was up.   I inquired, after 10 days in agony and not wasting words, "What the crap are you doing here, man?"

I had no illusions that he was bringing me flowers, and I was a week past patience for the pain, or any hope at all that it would ever end. At this point, death was the only sure release. His words were few, and he may have had to wipe a tear away before speaking. What he said had a kind of undesired authority, "Roll over on your side. This is going in your ass. It'll work quick, or it won't work at all."

That was the moment of truth. The bowel obstruction had all but killed me, if this didn't work, they would call my family in to say goodbye. I had felt worse than death for longer than I could remember. Well, he was right, it didn't take long. I barely made it to the bathroom before everything exploded out of me all at once. Nurses came to the room to check on me as they could hear from a distance what was going on. I was told not to close the bathroom door, so I left it open.

I remember a nurse peaking in my room for no more than a second, and then I heard her yelling down the hallway for all the staff to hear, "IT WORKED. IT WORKED. HE SHIT!"

Everyone there knew my story, and everyone had been extremely worried about me. And just like that, the hardest part was behind me! Or under me…

In the next couple of days, I was fitted with my first prosthetic leg. A week later, I was walking Jessica down the aisle at St. Wenceslaus Church, in my hometown, New Prague. The wedding was surreal. I was walking around in the body of a 20-year-old War Hero. But unknown to me, my mind was put together like that of a child, and it would take a solid decade to even become aware of that. Add to that, the fact that most of the memories from my childhood had been erased in the blast. The people who approached me were like ghosts the first time I met them. I was aware that I knew them, but the backstory, the context, was missing. No one would first say the phrase "brain injury" for still many years. I had no idea I was affected.

After the wedding, I felt like I had accomplished my first goal. Now all my energy was focused on snowboarding, and I had almost zero down time.

Before I got out of the hospital, I got a phone call from the Minnesota Vikings football team. They had a game that night against their rivals, the cheeseheads from Wisconsin, the  Packers. Yuck! They asked me if I would be their guest and co-captain for the game. This meant that I would stand on the field for the coin toss.

I took them up on the offer, and soon, there I was standing on a prosthetic leg for maybe the 6th or 7th time between two giants. To my left was Daunte Culpepper, to my right, Randy Moss.

They announced my name, and the entire stadium rose to their feet. The sound was deafening as they all greeted me at once.

I do not possess the vernacular to describe this feeling. I got to experience what these guys feel when 50,000-100,000 people put their positive intentions on you, and I have to say that the feeling is palpable. It is visceral, and it is real.

Just then, Daunte looked over and considerably down at me and patted my back just as they put us both up on the Jumbo Tron. At this point, I think I weighed right around 100 pounds, and I was new to my prosthetic leg, so the strong "pat on the back" from Daunte sent me flying forward.

The entire crowd witnessed this on the big screen and booed him relentlessly. This went on for what seemed like too long. The crowd did not stop booing him until I waved to them that I was okay. Daunte never made eye contact with me again. I commanded the will of more than 50,000 Minnesotans with the wave of my hand. That may be the single coolest thing that I've ever done.

When I was ready, I was released directly to the care of my mom. This was not normal, but I didn't go to what would be called a WTU. The standard practice for the Army quickly became to send injured soldiers to what was called a WTU, Warrior Transition Unit. These types of units are supposed to teach you about getting back to civilian life. In fact, I side-stepped any and all reintegration training, because someone in my command thought I would do best at my mom's house, in her always loving care. I had a lot of help.

I would never stand in formation again. December was only a week away. When I got out of the hospital, Kirk had already purchased my ticket to Colorado. I was finally going to see the mountains that Dad had talked about so lovingly. I knew I couldn't go there completely green. I was determined to show them a working plan when I got there.

I was injured August 29th, I walked Jessica down the aisle in October, and my first day back on snow was November 29th. Ski Spec started on December 2, but I had already gotten a hold of my old boss at Buck Hill, and boy was Jeff surprised to hear from me. I told him that I wanted to try to snowboard on my prosthetic leg.

His reply was simple. "Keith, are you going to hurt yourself? Are you going to hurt anyone else?"

I told him that I would learn to stop first thing. That's all it took; Jeff gave me a lift ticket on the house.

My first day back on snow, I was wearing my old gear including full pants. This hid my injury. That may have been the hardest part, because I was used to owning that hill. I was used to being admired on the hill. But that day I was pitied. It took a while to limp over to the center lift, the longest lift. My good leg strapped into the board, I used my prosthetic leg to skate with, but I was far short of graceful. I rode my own chair, and when I got close to the top, I signaled to the lifty to slow the thing down. The slight incline off the lift was my first challenge. I went straight down to my butt and slid out of the way of others as soon as possible. That is where I stayed for what could have been a couple of hours.

I was not sure how I would get down what now looked like a Colorado Black Diamond from my point of view. It was starting to get dark and the lights were already on when I took off from the top. Speed was immediate, and the only way to slow myself was to sit down. By the time I made it to the bottom, I was devastated. I was in tears being fully aware that it would never be the same. I could not extend my knee. I could only sit down and had to use my arms pushing against the hill to get back up. But already then. I was immediately going way too fast.

Although I was initially upset, thinking back, the hardest part was already behind me. I got an idea. I learned how to lock the knee straight so it could not bend. This did not make riding easy. But the knee didn't buckle when it was locked. Then I shortened the leg as much as I could. With these few developments, I made it down the hill. By the time I went to Ski Spec, I felt ready to show everyone at Breckenridge that I was going to do it. That I was going to keep snowboarding.

Chapter 13

I have often asked myself, "What is the best part about missing a leg?" I enjoy bringing levity to the situation, so I often tell people, "It's the parking."

But after I consider the question at length, the answer rises to the top like cream. The best part has been meeting the people that dedicate their lives to helping others. These are truly the richest people that I have ever met. And the best part about these people is that they all want to share with everyone they meet. My point is this, it took more than one person to get the sport of Paralympic Snowboarding off the ground. There were more than a few big players. Not all of them were disabled or even athletes themselves.

Ski Spec is hosted by an organization that I cannot call enough attention to. Kirk Bauer's organization, Disabled Sports USA, is the largest nonprofit in the United States dedicated to recovery through sport. Their mission is to provide national leadership and opportunities for individuals with disabilities to develop independence, confidence, and fitness through participation in community sports, recreation, and educational programs. Since 1967, Disabled Sports USA has focused on one goal: To improve the lives of wounded warriors, youth and adults with disabilities by providing sports and recreation opportunities. Disabilities include those with visual impairments, amputations, spinal cord injury, multiple sclerosis, head injury, cerebral palsy, other neuromuscular/orthopedic conditions, autism and related intellectual disabilities.

That first year at Ski Spec for me and other veterans was about getting back up on snow and about celebrating the fact that we were still alive. Already having figured out the ins and outs of my prosthesis, I was comfortable calling my progress that first year a success.

With that confidence on the mountain, my own self-confidence returned as well. The first year at Ski Spec, we had a lot of fun. One night all the participants were down in the bar. We were having a great time and drinking enough alcohol to become newly confident again. On my way to the bathroom that was just outside the bar and past the elevators, I noticed a sign hanging above the elevator buttons. It said, "Bachelorette party upstairs, room….", and that gave me an idea.

So, after I used the restroom, I went to search out a good-looking man named Matt Feeny. Matt used a wheelchair, and he was quite debonair. If I could convince him it would sway the crowd. I pitched the idea.

"Hey Feeny, there are a bunch of single women upstairs right now…Discount strippers?"

As I raised an eyebrow and lowered my chin, now a wide eyed slightly grinning nod…Feeny's face lit up like a Christmas tree. I removed my shirt as we knocked on the door. Before they answered, I had just enough time to get nervous, but there was no time for that. They answered the door quickly, and as they did, I asked them, without leaving time for discomfort, "DID SOMEBODY ORDER DISCOUNT STRIPPERS?"

We were received with an abundance of laughter and excitement. The crew of 5 or 6 of us followed the ladies around all night. We rode in their limo. We hit the town.

That first year at Ski Spec was not based on practical advances in adaptive snowboarding, but I made most of the connections that I would come to rely on that first year. I made a lot of important friends.

One of those friends had a link to the Sun Valley Adaptive Training Center in Idaho. The center was at the Sun Valley Ski Resort. I was invited there to keep advancing my riding. They rolled out the red carpet. The people at Sun Valley gave me my first hope that riding would get better if I kept with it. Riding with a straight back leg that could never bend was not a great way to ride, and I could not go very fast while in control. I'm not sure if my instructors wanted me to be able to go faster like I was asking for, or if they were afraid of what I would do if I continued at my current speed with such a small level of control. But it was obvious to my instructor what needed to happen. He told me as a matter of fact, that I needed to be able to bend my back knee.

My response was probably something like, "DUH!"

We went to the base to the maintenance shed. He pulled out a shovel, and in five minutes, he had cut the spade off the end and adapted a way to bolt what was left of the shovel, the "cane" to my binding. Once he did that, riding was never the same. With a cane attached to my rear binding, I could use my right arm to stand back up after I flexed my knee. Now I could take the knee out of being locked and allow it to flex. I had no ability to extend it without my right arm, but this was an advancement, a mechanical advancement that increased my ability immediately.

I was invited back to Ski Spec again the next year, and I was excited to show off what we had come up with at Sun Valley. The second year at Ski Spec was bigger than the first. All the people I met the first year were back plus many more.

Dan Gale, a completely able-bodied man was, and I hope still is, disabled only by his crippling affection for the lovely, Ms. Amy Purdy, an actress, model, clothing designer, author, motivational speaker and PARA-SNOWBOARDER! Dan's unwavering devotion to Ms. Purdy was the tip of the spear as far as advancing our sport. His motivation was love, so there was no force in our existence that could stand up to it. Dan proudly exhibited his love by way of his daily activities. He founded Adaptive Action Sports and worked day and night for years on end. If Dan's love was the motivating factor, then his foundation, AAS, was the spearhead itself, and Dan wielded his spear with the tenacity of a man protecting his children. That is why I'd like to name Daniel Gale as the Father of Para-snowboarding, and his now wife, Amy Gale, as the Mother of our Sport. They organized us. They introduced us. They put up with us when I acted like a child. So, they became our parents. Snowboarding was and is still a part of their family. Dan brought us all into that, his family, and I'm very proud of my seat there, and of my friendship with the now, Mr. and Mrs. Gale.

From the moment that I met Dan, he was talking about the next thing that he was going to try and get us involved with. So, it is no surprise, that he would team up with another man already shaking things up in the then named "Adaptive Snowboarding" world. By the time AAS came onto the scene, Lucas Grossi had already been snowboarding on a prosthetic leg for many years. Lucas is now and always was a leader. When we first met, he was the guy making the contacts necessary to get us racing. Lucas is the one that first got adaptive snowboarding accepted into races. The United States Snowboard Association is the largest Pro-Am series of snowboard races in the US. They host races coast to coast. With Lucas's help, everyone that Dan was making contacts with was also connected with Lucas.

So just like that, Adaptive Snowboarding was a real thing. We were off to the races. For the first time in history, we spoke of disabled athletes competing in snowboarding races against other disabled athletes. Lucas is still making dreams happen every day with his current venture, Dream Adaptive. Their mission is to enhance the quality of life of individuals with disabilities by providing year-round outdoor adaptive recreational opportunities.

The second year at Ski Spec, I was introduced to a man named, Jerm Fry. After Jerm lost his leg, he missed his favorite activity so much that he decided to design and build a prosthetic knee that would allow him to continue it, to telemark ski. This is an advanced type of skiing used to traverse extremely steep terrain. This type of skiing commands the full flexion and powered extension of both legs. What Jerm invented was a mechanical coil over-shock system to fit into a custom-built knee chassis. Just seeing this knee gave me instantaneous hope. It represented the first time that I would be able to put on pants and ride like any other common "Jabroni" on the mountain. Up to this point, I had to use the cane which meant answering the same question every time I entered the lift line. Everyone there always wanted to know why I was using it.

Jerm's knee, the XT9, changed my life. If I carried anything but VA insurance, I would never have stood a chance to get one of these legs, because of the politics involved. Jerm was so excited to see it work for me, that he never asked for it back. He claimed that the VA would cover its cost before I ever asked them to. It was not because they had to, but because I figured that they wanted to. And they did.

The truth is that the United Stated VA has been aiding the advancement of athletic prosthesis nearly exclusively for as long as US service men have been fighting wars…Long enough I'd say.

From the first time that I put it on, my new prothesis was amazing. I was standing, I could put weight over my back leg again and ride square over my board. I could absorb the terrain of the mountain allowing me to get brave again. Within seconds of standing up, I was free. I was flying. I was at Big Sky with the good man learning to ride all over again. And just like that, I was in LOVE with riding all over again.

Chapter 14

Two other people that are close to the top of the list of influential people that I met in the early days are David Pool and Nicole Roundy. I first met David at a mid-summer training session hosted at the world famous Windells Snowboarding Camp. This was organized by AAS with help from Lucas Grossi. It had to be August. David was wearing sunglasses with his zip up sweater open exposing his chest to the hot August sun. He sat perched in his sit ski, which is what it sounds like, a bucket seat on top of a ski. David is paraplegic. He was looking confidently over his line. He was waiting in line to hit the jumps in the terrain park.

As I slid to a stop behind him, I introduced myself. My shorts made my leg visible, so it was obvious to me that we were both likely attending the same camp, but we hadn't met yet. I still hadn't taken the XT9 off any big jumps or booters, however, I had convinced myself that this was the day. As I introduced myself, David looked me up and down.

After he had taken me in, he waited a second, he paused, then he said clearly with a stone-cold look on his face, "Will you take my line?"

In that second, I decided to go big; to go as big as I could and let the cards fall where they may. I don't remember speaking an answer. I gave David a nod just as the course cleared. He did not bother looking back to see if I was behind him. He didn't "wash" speed either. Sit skiers can push using their outriggers, and David was still pushing up the approach.

Before he hit the first lip, I was off to catch him, and I was also thrown back in the fight. I was sheriff, Rosco P Coldtrain in "hot pursuit" of them Duke boys, and I was about to launch over the creek.

I saw him approach and hit boot #2 as I was in the air from #1. He was still charging. I had never hit anything on the big side of the park, but I wasn't about to let David get away. David was SENDING IT off the money booter, by the time I hit #2. Both of his outriggers were exuberantly extended in the air.

Then it was my turn. My blood was pumping, my heart was racing, and I was now doing at least 60 mph headed over the top of a 50-foot table. I could tell as soon as I left the lip, that I would make the landing, so I confidently reached for the tip of my board grabbing it to stabilize myself in the air. Landing, I already saw David cheering me on.

By the end of that week, I was spinning 360s off those little jumps, and I had made another life-long friend. Thanks Pool boy.

That was also around the same time that I met Nicole Roundy. Nicole was the first female above knee Para-snowboarder, that I knew of. She was/is my age, and she is cute! I always enjoyed chasing Roundy around the mountain. Nicole also wore the XT9 and spent a lot of her time carving out a place for our sport. Nicole is now one of the most heavily medaled para-snowboarders in the world, and I am very proud to call her my friend.

Chapter 15

If I remember correctly, I started competing again sometime around 2007. That's right. I woke up from a 10-day long rest in Las Vegas after I wrecked my motorcycle on my way to school one day, and with my family surrounding me, we decided that it was time for me to leave Vegas and move to Colorado. There I started snowboarding nearly immediately. I rented houses in the mountains every winter and then moved to Denver in the summer to save on rent and to go kayaking.

Living in Blue River all winter at above 10,000 feet in elevation was good conditioning.

After sleeping there for a month, there was no place on earth I was not conditioned to ride. While I was living above Breck, I rode nearly every day.

       I roomed with a pair of brothers that I met while I was training at Windells. Those guys were nuts. In case anyone remembers this, I don't remember their names. But these guys were crazy. One night the power went out in Breckenridge, and these boys actually looted. They claimed to have broken windows and grabbed merchandise out of stores. I was unsure when to believe what they were telling me, and it's not important. Those brothers and I rode every day and together we shared some lively times.

       Then out of the blue, I got a call from the people at Glamour Magazine, and I was invited to an A-List party. It was my first, and I was excited. They were hosting an event in NYC at Carnegie Hall. Cher was to be honored and given a lifetime achievement award, and I was to present her with it.

Miss Lindsay Vohn was to accept her athlete of the year award. I was wearing my Class A uniform, and I was feeling confident. At the party, I was accompanied by

another soldier. He wore high rank and patches that didn't make sense to me. His experiences were the kind that you see in the movies. In a situation like that, it is appropriate for a prior soldier to share what they are comfortable with or what they are allowed to share. After hearing what he had to say, I knew better than to ask any further questions.

At this event, we shared hugs with Oprah and Fergie. Whoever that is! Fergie had the most security surrounding her, at a party, and I found that pretentious.

Also, I ran into the lovely Miss Vohn. I was double fisting Jack and Cokes. Socially lubricated and looking good, I approached with an abundance of confidence. I put one of my drinks in her hand as if I had gotten it for her.

I said simply, "Lindsay, I'm Keith. I also grew up riding. Buck Hill."

I'll never forget her response. Lindsay said, "If you can turn on ice you can turn on anything."

After a little further conversation, Mr. GI Joe himself, Josh Duhamel, walked up and stole her attention from me. Let me tell you why. He is a huge, good-looking man. Yeah sure, "The Rock" Johnson makes him look small in those movies, but that is because "The Rock" is a giant human being. Josh stands well over 6 feet tall.

I had the most fun the entire evening keeping Kelly Osborne away from my drinks. I hear she is doing well now, but in those days, she was a loosely closeted drinker.

I recall Kelly shouting in her British accent to us as she was pulled away towards the end of the evening, "Keith, meet us at the Boom Boom Room."

Now, I have no idea what that is, and my girlfriend had just fallen off the curb drunk, so we went back to the hotel.

Chapter 16

I now had the VA supporting my efforts 100%, and with people like Kirk, Dan, and Lucas founding organizations filled with volunteers all banding together to tackle the politics, all I had to do was ride my snowboard as often as I could. I managed that nearly every day. Including travel, I remember riding at or around 300 days a year in those days. It is what we did every day, and that was beyond my wildest dreams as a child. It was my job to snowboard. I had made it.

I have been heli-dropped at the peak of my choice and ridden snow that I never knew the depth of. I've been towed up the mountain behind snowmobiles in front of thousands of screaming fans at venues like the Winter X Games and other World Championship events the world over.

In New Zealand, we competed in the Audi Quatro Games.

I have never enjoyed myself more than I did in New Zealand.

I highly recommend you attend those games if you are able. That has been my favorite place on earth so far.

I also have met so many of my childhood heroes in the sport. I'm happy that I was involved with the sport before it became a business, as I believe as I have stated before, I was not cut out to be a professional. I just tried as hard as they did and feel lucky now, as I reminisce, for being allowed to keep their company. I acted like a child most of the time, as entire regions of my brain were still in early stages of development following the blast that took my leg. But I did always shine at the after party. In high school, I was voted the "best party thrower" in my class. Since my brain injury, I have learned to calm down a little bit, but I still know how to have a good time.

There were a few moments in those years where my abilities took a great leap. A couple of them happened at Ski Spec. Developing the cane allowed me to stand on my board. This was necessary to ride with speed and control. But this had its problems. The cane did not allow the use of my leg. It allowed me to work while standing. But I worked around my bum leg in those days.

With the advancement of prosthetic knees like the XT9, my abilities took additional great leaps. Snowboarding didn't start out easy, by any means. The biggest problem that I had with my cane was social… I was constantly answering the same question in the lift line about the "cane" attached to my binding. However, with the use of it, I was not just making it down the mountain, I was catching air over bumps and looking for more speed on any blue run.

Then Mom helped me answer all the questions in the lift line before they were asked. She took my pair of pants, cut off my right leg at the knee and hemmed a piece of elastic in so they would seal against my socket.

This left my prosthetic leg exposed to the elements and visible to everyone else, and just like that, instead of people clowning my cane they were all giving me props. Suddenly, I had the confidence of the Little Engine That Could. "I think I can! I think I can! I think I can!" No one ever stopped me. How could I stop? Everyone I saw gave me a thumbs up!

The next year at Ski Spec, I showed up ready to race. I was excited to show off how much I had improved to the largest gathering of disabled athletes in the world. That year was BIG! Everyone was impressed to see how well I was riding. That triggered invitations to go ride at other places. I went to Snow Mass for a week to ski with disabled vets with their adaptive program. I have been to Tahoe more than a couple times. I was riding for fun again, and I was riding the most beautiful places in the country. Every day was a fairy tale. I woke up and only considered how I could improve my snowboarding. How could I go faster?

I was lucky to ride some cool places back then. But the best part was always the people and the parties. There was always a filet and an open bar. I'd like to say I behaved appropriately, but the opposite is true. The truth is that in those days I always had a pocket full of Benzos, and I also had a drinking habit. Benzodiazepines mixed with alcohol make the inhibition from alcohol alone look like child's play. Truly absurd. The things I did will follow me for the rest of my life, and I don't think I will ever live them down, but I didn't know any better at the time and I do now. So its hard to regret.

The XT9 did not exist before Jerm built it. And no insurance company on the planet would have ever purchased it if the VA didn't do it first, because of the liability involved with an already disabled person getter further injured. The XT9 was tunable. It was not all roses; however, I could adapt it to work better for me in a variety of situations.

I recall trying every spring rate that I could get my hands on. At one point, I threw in a 450 or 500 lb. spring before I settled on a 350 lb. dual rate unit. That is what I would wear today if I wanted to go retro. But the 500 lb. spring was the most fantastic of all that I tried.

Imagine this… You are doing 65-70 mph on a racecourse looking for more speed anywhere you can get it. On your approach to the money booter at the end of the race, you find the only spot of slush on the entire course. The slush strips speed like sandpaper, and the result is a 15-mph hit. You no longer carry enough speed to clear the table, nor do you have the time to avoid it, so you are now sailing 25 feet in the air with nothing under you but flat ground. I made the conscious choice that day to blow it up. I had done it before. I would just position my weight over my prosthetic, and land on it. This would surely grenade it. It wouldn't be pretty, but it would save my good knee.

That's why I carried two XT9s. I rode a snowmobile down the mountain many times a year in the early days, always with a smile. But not that day! That 500 lb. spring had another idea. Imagine the carnage involved when a 130-pound man falling from 25 feet in the air fully compresses a 500 lb. spring leaving only the 130-pound man above the now fully compressed 500 lb. spring. Fantastic carnage! One side of my body wanted to launch into space and the other side was not happy to be connected to the same snowboard. I survived, but I took the rest of the day off.

Lucas showed his leadership when he introduced me to Jerm, and our relationship made it possible for above knee amputees to first purchase an XT9. When I met Lucas, he had already teamed up with Adaptive Action Sports (AAS), led by Daniel Gale. As I have told you, Dan was enamored with Amy Purdy, who some of you may recognize from her appearance on

"Dancing with the Stars." Amy was the beautiful, 20 something, redhead who lost her feet to meningitis as a teenage girl. Dan fell for Amy as hard as I imagine a man can fall for a woman. I was always and still am a bit of a flirt, but Amy was always off limits. Dan had dibbs from the start, and he didn't even have to say it. His efforts said it all.

Adaptive Action Sports was the tip of the spear as far as organizations paving the way for competitive adaptive snowboarding, and Dan's efforts to organize the sport in those early days were both founding and profound. Dan made contacts with the biggest names in the industry. Dan got us invited to Windells to train at Mt. Hood in the middle of summer.

He partnered with Lucas, who got us invited to race at any and all USASA races, and the USASA is big. These people host races nationwide at almost every resort and ski hill. Dan put me in the gates next to Sean White,

and he first got us invited to international competitions. Then Dan got us invited to the Winter X Games. Dan would have stopped time, if that's what Amy told him he had to do. But that's not what happened. I like to think that the moment Adaptive Snowboarding became Paralympic Snowboarding is the night that Amy told Dan that her old dream of snowboarding in the Olympics had been shattered. It's a romantic idea, but Dan is a pretty romantic guy. He developed the sport of Paralympic snowboarding to show his love for Amy.

I think it was the 2008 USASA National Competition. The setting was beautiful North Lake Tahoe, one of my favorite places in the USA. My friend, Tyler Mosher, and I were walking around the village after a long day of competing. Tyler is a Canadian Professional Adaptive Snowboard Racer. He was perhaps the oldest adaptive rider back in the day. He may have been the first one at it. I spoke to him about what made him keep snowboarding after his injury, and he told me he never really considered not riding. His recovery was like mine and similar to most of the athletes that I talked to. He just wanted to get back on snow, and he did it as fast as he could.

Tyler had already been racing for years and always represented stout competition. Back in those days, there was no classification. We raced each other head to head, and that was fun. Today, a below knee amp would never race an above knee amp, because someone might get their feelings hurt. As if that matters. That would never have happened back in the good old days. I never once considered winning important, as long as I was invited to the next race. I wanted snowboarding to be available to the next guy. I was totally aware that I was riding the leading edge of the sport, and it was nothing short of my wildest dreams coming true.

Tyler and I were probably getting a beer or just about to start relaxing. The village at the base was packed with people already staging themselves for the medal's ceremony after the competition. I had already switched into my C-Leg, (bionic leg) but I was wearing shorts, a race bib, and I was carrying my XT9 in my hand. Suddenly a youngster headed my direction. Once this boy, Chance, spotted my knee, he B-lined straight for me.

The best part about children is their unbiased honesty. Chance walked right up and already in his approach, I grabbed his mother's attention with my eyes, and using only our eyebrows, we managed to communicate that it was okay to tell him my story. When he asked what happened, I told him that I had been a soldier. When he asked how I lost my leg. I told him it was an RPG. When he asked what that was, I told him it was a Rocket Propelled Grenade. I could see the wheels in Chance's head spinning as he considered what to ask me next. And then a sudden look of innocent confusion washed over him. He tugged on Tyler's sleeve and asked Tyler, in a low voice as if he were embarrassed to ask me, "What's worse, a rocket or a grenade?"

Tyler shrugged his shoulders and responded without much thought, "I don't know kid, they both kill people."

As if he was in disbelief of what Tyler had told him, he looked up at Tyler without missing a beat and scoffed a little as he thumbed in my direction and said defiantly and loud enough for me to hear, "Huh, didn't kill this guy."

I think this was the greatest single moment of my life. Thanks Chance! If I ever get lucky enough to have a little boy, I'll do my best to name him Chance.

I was fortunate to race around the world, under big lights, and I even won a few races.

Not many. But not even a medal from the President, made me feel like I did when Chance made his comment. Chance made me feel like Superman. Thanks, little bud. Keep charging!

I'll refer to those years as the good old days: '07, '08, '09, 10. I got to race in the Winter X games in three of those years. I'll never forget the athletes' tent at the X Games. Red Bull girls were serving me as I sat in a massage chair playing video games. Paparazzi wanted pictures. I even got harassed by a good-looking reporter. I was having a drink at the athletes' bar and talking with one of my old idols from the early days of boarder cross. This guy was kind of the bad boy of the sport back in the day, and I was having a hard time believing that I was talking to him. Then a gorgeous girl sat down with us. She didn't ask permission, as beautiful women are to do. She immediately asked who we were, and she was very interested. I took the opportunity to chat her up, as I was alone that weekend, or at that point anyways. But my boy put a sure and quick stop to that. He cut right to the chase and asked her what she thought she was doing in there. He told her she wasn't allowed to be there, and that he would get her removed if she didn't leave on her own. I cracked a huge smile as soon as I heard the tone in his voice. And by the time he finished his thought, I was laughing loudly. I could not make eye contact with the poor girl. Although my remorse was short lived. She quickly left the table with her head down, and he explained to me that she was a reporter.

He said that he couldn't stand when pretty girls think they can do whatever they want. YES! I was in the right company. This guy was my hero, and I liked him because I read stories of him acting just like this. Now I'm telling a similar story involving my old hero. That was one of the top moments of my career.

I ride far better today than I ever did with two legs. I won't say that I'm grateful to have lost my leg, but I will say that I would do it again. Pain is temporary, and all of life is filled with pain. If we live life in fear of pain, we make irrational decisions. All pain is temporary. Therefore, I fear nothing.

Chapter 17

With national recognition came attention. So, in the fall of 2009, I was approached by an organization that claimed they were poised to write a large grant and fund what would become the first US Paralympic snowboarding team. This organization told me directly that they needed my cooperation as the grant they were applying for was supposed to be used to train injured service men and women. At least that's how they explained it to me in order to get me involved. It was obvious as soon as I became involved, that was not their intention. I was given a room to stay at in the basement of a hotel in the area, which was great. But I was finishing up a degree in Denver, so I mostly stayed in the city. Working with this organization, we decided on and hired a coach to train the team. I maintained a workout schedule at the gym up there. But living in Denver and commuting to practice every day was hard. As a matter of fact, it nearly killed me.

On my way up to the mountain one morning, while ride sharing with another athlete, Lacey, the photogenic one,

she hit some ice and rolled her boyfriend's 4runner, with us inside. Right off the side of the mountain.

Luckily, after 3 or 4 complete rolls, we hit a tree that stopped us. I remember it like it was yesterday. We came around an icy corner and her backend broke loose. I was already acting like a man and telling her not to overcompensate when she did. When we hit the railing, time was ticking slowly, and I remember saying something like, "We're going to be fine." We were lucky that his car was clean. Objects in a rolling car can become projectiles. It must have taken a while to get the Forerunner out. I am just glad we walked away unharmed.

We were late to practice that day. But that was nothing new for me. Living two hours away and fighting traffic to the mountain most days meant that I was often late, on school nights anyways. After only a few times arriving late, the one other athlete on the team got frustrated with waiting, so he and the coach more or less ignored me for the rest of the season. I was left to ride on my own. The other athlete and the coach shared a like injury and so had a lot in common. I am happy that they got close.

I remember my first international competition. It was in Whistler in British Columbia, Canada. I drove my Jeep up there, because I couldn't afford a place to stay, and I was mostly on my own at this point.

Everyone there was talking about classification. For the first time, we would be classified as different because of our injuries. Would I be given a head start over some of the other "less disabled" athletes? Would there be any one "more disabled" than me? And would they really call it "handicap snowboarding"? I paid little attention to it. I've never begged a day in my life. The accommodations in the early days were often bleak; money was always tight, so I did what I had to do. I was just happy for the invite.

I had already completed my first two laps in Whistler, and I put down 2 times. However, I was not satisfied, so I decided on the gondola ride up for my last run that I was going to charge hard for it. And charge I did. I don't remember finishing that race. But I remember everything but the finish. I was coming out of the last berm hot, too hot to hit the last table with that much speed. At this rate, it looked like I would take out the finish line banner suspended above the finish line. But my mind was made up. I wanted the time. I charged anyway. I don't know why, but as I left the lip of that last table, I looked back over my front shoulder. And that's all it took, before I knew what happened, I was facing up the mountain, and I was sailing past the finish line completely backwards. The first thing to touch the ground was the back edge of my snowboard. The second thing was the back of my head. At race speed, maybe 70 mph; I never fell harder. That was one of the worst concussions of my life.

I woke up in the Snow-cat on my way to the hospital. After hours of waiting impatiently in a neck brace, I was told that I stretched my optic nerve and that my vision may return to normal eventually. I was seeing double everywhere I looked. Regular vision returned while I slept about 6 months later.

At a competition in France, our "coach" forgot to book me a room for the last night of our trip. I was told, "Oops, it was a mistake! You'll need to find a couch to crash on!" So, I did, but I also let my "coach" know that I didn't appreciate anything that he had done, and that if I had anything to say about it that he was done.

Today, my regards for that man are not high. I suppose he played his part. But the guy had us wearing golf shoes in our bindings. We looked like fools. In my opinion the man was in no way qualified to begin with, and that was my fault as I played a key role in choosing him. Here is where we went wrong. As a world class disabled athlete, I don't need to chase a disabled old man. He was not hard to keep up with. A lot of the time I felt like he needed more help than I did. As an emerging athlete I needed to be challenged, I needed someone that I could chase. However, this guy's best days were already long behind him.

No matter the situation, my riding improved dramatically. Being left behind and left out of training by the team most days meant that I rode by myself or with friends that came to the mountain. That was fine with me. The pass was still covered, or so I thought.

I found bumps to be challenging, so I spent most days riding bumpy trees. The consequence was high in the trees. That sharpened my focus. Eventually I learned that they weren't too bad after a fresh few inches, and although I never totally got the hang of them, my riding and control during my time there grew by leaps and bounds. Although the political turmoil ran deep, this was the peak of my snowboarding career.

At competitions, I stayed away from the American team. I was always afraid to get yelled at, and even more afraid of what I would say to someone if they attempted to reprimand me. I was as afraid of what would come out of my mouth as everyone else.

However, the first thing I always did upon entering a new country was always to learn to say, "please" and "thank you." I was always quick to make international friends. With those two phrases there are few places that even an American will not be welcomed. I have never claimed to be Canadian while I travel like I see a lot of Americans doing.

The rest of the American team would have to be brave to say anything to me, and so no one did. We competed together like estranged kin. There was one exception. To my coach I was a slacker. I got on the team because I was needed for the grant and I think because he made that assumption, he also assumed that I had no heart, no chips in the bet, that I had nothing riding on the outcome of the competitions. His perspective was that I was just along for the ride. I suppose he would have had a solid point if I would have been willing to listen to him.

That is until we were in the gates at the X games one year for our practice run. We would be given 15 minutes to ride the course in order to get to know it once before the race. We all dropped out of the gates at once. The gate was a ledge about 12 feet above a quarter pipe that was the start of the race surface. 0 to 50 mph, NOW was more than a challenge for me, and I fell on my first attempt. I immediately took off my board and climbed the hill back to the gate to take a second attempt. I paid no attention to what everyone else was doing. Although I was not the only one to fall, I was the only one not to continue to look at the rest of the course. It was obvious to me that if I could not manage to get out of the gates that I had little chance to win the race. I kicked toe holes and climbed back up to the gates. Along the way, the guy calling himself coach grabbed my snowboard and carried it up the mountain for me. On the short way back up to the gate, he actually complimented my "heart" and told me that I was doing the right thing.

At my most recent race in New Zealand, it was obvious that nothing had changed. I found one of my binding screws loose right before a race, when I was already at the top of the mountain. I begrudgingly found a US coach (an over-weight man that I had never met) and requested a tool to tighten my binding. Then the asshole told me that his tools were "too fragile to lend them out." Quickly, he facetiously apologized for being an ass hole.

I quickly responded, "It's nobody's fault, but yours!"

Just then a man from what must have been the Chinese team approached me and tugged on my sleeve. He had watched the entire thing, and he was laughing at us as he handed me a wrench. I was never more embarrassed to be wearing old glory.

That was my last competition. Maybe I never had what it took to be a professional. But I always had enough friends, even if we did have trouble communicating. That year on the team was a big one. We also raced in France in the Alps. The mountain was gorgeous. This would be the race where I would contribute more the night before the race than on the racecourse.

I fled the company of anyone wearing red, white and blue as soon as I was granted my freedom as was standard practice by this point. I could not stand to be around the American team. Everyone else in the world was still enchanted with and excited by the new opportunity. The US team was already structuring the sport professionally, which was inevitable, I suppose. But I wanted no part of it. I was too busy living the active celebration. That's really why I never made it. The sport went from a celebration and demonstration of what we could do, to a concentration on professionalism, and that change was too much for me. I was not at a place in my mental and emotional recovery where I could make that happen.

My greatest contribution to the team in France came the night before the race.

All the rest of the Americans were good professional racers, so they were in

bed early to get a good night's rest, except for David Pool and me. We started the evening drinking buffet wine by the "liter" in the board tuning room in the basement of the hotel. Before I knew it, other athletes from around the world joined in. By the end of the night, we were arm locked and 30 strong. We sang each other's anthems while shooting flaming Sambuca. We closed every bar in the village that night.

I barely made it to the race the next morning, which was around noon. The prior night's festivities were likely my biggest contribution to the team. As Pool and I may have aided and persuaded to lowering the bar for everyone else. But man did we have a blast. I enjoyed France. Those yellow-bellied surrender monkeys really know how to party. Just a little lighthearted international banter. We always got your back France, don't worry.

As USASA Nationals approached again, the season came to an end. However, there was still one more big advancement to take place. There was to be a new athlete at Nationals this year. His name was Mike Shultz, and he was an AK (above knee amputee) like me. He was riding with a brand-new knee, that he invented in his garage. He designed it so that he could continue his favorite sport of racing snowmobiles at a pinnacle level. Mike is a professional racer. He had been before he lost his leg, and the loss of his leg never slowed him down. After 13 days in the hospital, Mike was released, and he had already designed a way to continue what he loved. And so, the day before the 2010-2011 national's competition, I first strapped on Mikes creation, the "Moto knee."

The next day, I was crowned the fasted adaptive snowboarder in the country, racing on Mike's new knee. The Moto Knee was tremendous. It was equal to the advancement I felt when I first strapped on the XT9. In fact, they are similar knees except the Moto knee uses a more advanced shock unit that dampened movement in both directions. In addition, riding (moving) top ram position allows for a custom tunable flection profile. Working with Mike was surreal. Ideas went straight to manufacture. The unit was tunable with only an air pump.

The political interference ran deeper than I ever imagined, however. At the end of the 2010-11 season, I was the reigning national champion in the brand-new sport of "adaptive snowboarding," that I helped to carve a place for. It was a sport that was now sure to debut at the upcoming 2012 games in Sochi, Russia. I was the number one ranked athlete in the US. I had the world's best health insurance behind me, and they kept me in the most cutting-edge prosthesis, of which I have now been able to help in the development of the leading two. I was now riding better than ever. Better even than I did with two legs. And so, from a high place, I had far to fall.

Chapter 18

The organization that had agreed to cover the cost of my training and competition season left me with a huge bill at the end of that year, and my now ex-wife was keeping a secret as well. She would have fit in perfectly on that cable show where we all laugh at the women who claim they were unaware of their pregnancy. She didn't gain a lot of weight and always had an excuse for any discomfort. Hm… Until one day, after spending hours in the bathroom, she told me that we needed to go to the hospital and that she didn't know why. As we walked in, a nurse guided us to the delivery room without even asking why we were there, it was then, that I first learned that I would be a dad in the next few minutes. I think my daughter almost fell out. Man, were we not ready! If you love each other, you are ready. We didn't have that. Everything we had was a lie.

There is nothing in my experience that I am more grateful for than my daughter. No matter the initially perceived cost, I am confident that having her saved my life. And although I did not know she was coming. It was clear what I had to do.

With the help from an old friend, I was invited to a gala. The SEAKR foundation had been taking care of the family of my fallen squad leader, SSG. Mark A. Lawton, since his death. This year MG Collins was to speak at their annual gala, and I was invited to sit at the head table. There I met my new bosses.

I spent the next 6 years working in the booming aerospace defense industry. There I took part in building everything from bombs, to shuttle parts, to parts for the new James Web space telescope.

I worked in the test department. I am not sure what I am not supposed to talk about, and I have zero interest in putting my foot in my mouth, so that's all that I will say about my experience. I did not play any kind of key role there. In fact, I was probably the lowest paid person there. The truth is that I had a dream of becoming an aerospace engineer back before my dad passed away. Aerospace engineering was perhaps my first dream, and it too came true.

It's hard to think of a dream of mine that has not come true, whether by chance or by way of grit, but I had given up on that dream many times over since Dad's death. When I eventually found myself working in the industry, I was exposed to my old abandoned dream. It turned out there was very little of what I had imagined as a child involved. Exactly none on my part. It was often said that the paperwork that followed what we built was just as important as whatever it was that we built. This was something that I had no awareness of in my youth, and perhaps if nothing ever went wrong in my life, Dad still being alive, perhaps I would have chased my first dream. However, finding myself there after the world had thoroughly rung me out more than once already, I quickly felt sure that I was not cut out for that. I remember once asking someone for a hammer. The look that I got back would remind you of the look you might give a school bus driver with cigarette in their mouth, asking for a light. I did not belong there.

It was during this time that the new sport of Paralympic Snowboarding finally came to full bloom. 2016 was a repeat of 2012. I was just taking on a daytime role as the United States swept the podium for a second time. I did not participate in any way. I again cheered for my friends and new heroes from half a world away. I was proud to see Mike Shultz earn his medals.

Weeks turned to months, and months turned to years. Then one day, my now little girl, and I sat down for a little talk. I could understand her before she was a year old. Now here she was just the blink of an eye later holding an entire conversation. She was about to start first grade. This would mean full days at school with neither parent there with her. As we talked, I was asking her if she was comfortable enough to do it on her own, and she had a unique answer for me. When I asked her if she had enough friends to make it through the day. She told me that everyone was her friend, and that she didn't have any "not friends."

She told me she wanted to start a club for her friends that have trophies from winning something. She wanted to start a "Winners' Club" for all her friends that were "good at stuff." I could not contain my excitement. I was shaking. I was vibrating. I immediately told her that she had a great idea, and that I would do anything that I could to help her. Then her response changed the course of my life instantly. She told me that if I wanted to be in her club, that I would have to go and win more medals.

I guess I never noticed how closely she was listening while I talked about how I used to race, but I do remember my dad's face when he talked about skiing, like it was yesterday, and apparently, we had that in common. My daughter had already enjoyed her first day on a snowboard a

few years earlier. But what she said caught me off guard. I hadn't thought much about snowboarding since my daughter was born. Although we had already enjoyed many days on the Mt together. Breckenridge even honored us on her first day ever on snow by sharing the first chair of the season with us. Thanks, Breckenridge. That was unforgettable.

They even gave my princess, a private lesson. Her instructor had a "gold pass" meaning she was a twenty-year volunteer instructor.

I think maybe my daughter saw me get excited. But I hadn't even thought of racing in years. I was only 33 years old and still feeling pretty young, so I

told her that I would see what I could do.

      After that conversation, I made a phone call to an old friend asking about possible races. That call turned nearly immediately into more calls, and before I knew it, I was on my way around the world to my first competition since the birth of my little girl. She had requested that I win her a trophy, and now it was my duty to show her that there was nothing that I couldn't do if I really wanted to.

      I would need to bring her a trophy in order to be in her club, and that sounded great to me. It didn't matter that I hadn't ridden my snowboard 10 times since I last raced 6 years earlier. I would be able to bring her a trophy no matter what, as I could easily define anything as a trophy to my 5-year-old. Trophies are a literal metaphor of a memory that represents a victory. Easy stuff.

      It was during this trip, that I found my "happy place" and decided to start writing. This book is the culmination of the lesson that I set out to teach my daughter when I left my job in order to continue my vocation. My 5 year old daughter had called me out. She had told me in not so many words that I was not doing what I was supposed to be doing. At the end of the day, my little girl needs to know that there is nothing in this life that she cannot accomplish if she sets her mind to it, she makes a plan, and perseveres to the end. Also, that to be afraid is natural, but that fear contains vast volatile energy that needs to be focused and utilized to our advantage before it is allowed to hurt us, because fear can be transferred and expelled most directly as anger or passion. While holding on to anger can be like holding onto a hot stone with the intention to throw it at someone, fear can also be focused into passion, and enough fear-based passion in a single person can change the world. Understanding that took my entire life so far.

My darling girl,

Nothing is impossible. To fail, is to learn, is to one day succeed. Don't use the word, "can't," because You Can do anything you set your mind to. Your path may not always be clear or easy, but nothing good in life comes from easy indecision. You don't run from a fight, because it makes you look weak, and you are not. You stand up for what's right; because the person next to you may not be strong enough; it is your responsibility to protect them, because you are strong enough. At some point I lost the control that I once had over my emotions, and I will struggle to rebuild that. But you do not carry my excuse. My father told me before he died that he carried fear and regret over public speaking, and so I find comfort in conquering my fear of that. I hope for you that you learn a masterful control of your emotions, and I pray that you maintain them, as emotion is necessary for the greatest gift possessed by all of humanity; that is Empathy for one another.

Chapter 19

When I consider gratitude, as I often like to do, there are many people and groups that come to mind. First and Foremost, my courageous Mom, Judy Deutsch. After Dad died, Mom raised 5 kids. All of whom have become quite

Run New Prague 2018

successful. She dropped everything to join me after my injury and stood up for me when it would have been easier to say nothing.

Mom stands tall next to Dad as the two people that I should and need to model my life after. I have had great examples of how I should live shining throughout my life. None greater, none more essential to how I make daily decisions than my Mom and Dad.

To Disabled Sports USA and all their employees and volunteers, I prefer your company to any the world over.

To Dan and Amy Gale, I miss the good old days when were working actively to

we

change the world. I wish you all the success with your family that you have had in the rest of your lives.

To Lucas Grossi, I am appreciative of you for always leading the way. With your help, there was always a next race. To all the athletes like, from left to right; Evan Strong, Tyler Mosher, Dan Monzo, Mike Shea, and Ian Lockey, to include David Pool and Nicole Roundy, it was an honor to be in your company.

And perhaps the most influential group of all is the one that consists of 309,000 full time health care professionals, our nation's largest health care company, our nation's Veteran's Administration. The rest of this book will be dedicated to thanking each of those selfless miracle workers.

I spent the later part of September and the first weeks of October of 2003 in DC at Walter Reed. There the staff worked extremely long hours and showed up every single day with a full tank of hope, patience and love.

Throughout my stay, I had no doubt that I had the finest care the world over. Every single day what little bravery I had left was dwarfed by the nurses and doctors who entered my room every time it was necessary. They literally and figuratively picked me up off the floor many times, often out from a puddle of my own blood and waste. I was a stranger to these people, yet, each time, they smiled at me with a face of infinite caring. I couldn't understand where they found it. But I am so very grateful.

I was going to write a thank you to each of my prosthetists. The vast majority of whom have been inexplicably named, "Bill", then I was going to write a thank you to the staff at Walter Reed and everyone on the Amputee Ward. When I was there in 2003, those HEROES worked long days and faced picket lines as they left work, only to come back each day with another full tank of hope and motivation. It was nothing short of miraculous.

I'd like to thank the phone operators, who I'm sure hear the same story about memory loss each time they pick up the phone, for being patient and always letting me finish, even though they already knew how the story ends. I'm filled with gratitude for every nurse who I mouthed off to. You helped me find my personality again. Thanks also to the many occupational and recreational therapists who helped me realize that my injury represented so many opportunities. Thank you to the Las Vegas VA hospital crew for putting me back together after that bike wreck landed me in that coma. Thanks to the administration workers sitting in some office reading the reports of a young soldier breaking every prosthetic leg given to him immediately. Thank you for always giving me another one, and when what I asked for didn't exist, thank you for enabling the development of cutting-edge technology, simply because I requested it. To all 309,000 of you. Thank you for every smile of compassionate encouragement. Thank you for flirting with me when I hadn't eaten in two months and weighed 98 pounds. Thank you for always letting my visitors in no matter what time it was. Thank you for every extra piece of cake and jello, for every new pillow, for every cup of ice water and every time you brushed my teeth.

Thank You!

For 02:59!

Thank You!

Through my next finish Line!

For Never saying, "Never",

For Never saying, "Can't",

Always a new challenge.

You always led the chant.

You pushed me on to Victory.

The likes of which most never see.

My victory lap among the stars.

I even got to race fast cars.

MY DUTY NOW TO

THANK YOU!

And so, WITH ALL OF ME, I SAY.

Thank you for my three right feet,

my joy;

and your help to light my way.

I am Happy!

Glossary of Terms Used

Armor- A standard set of armor quickly became necessary to include bullet proof plates over the vital areas. When I left, I was wearing a flak jacket made in 1981. This was similar to the lead suit that you wear when you get an x-ray. It  saved my life.

Avenger-

BDUs- Battle Dress Uniform

DCUs- Desert Camouflage Uniform

Duffle- A soldier's duffle bag is used for gear. Depending on what you were doing I imagine this varied greatly. Mine carried armor.

Essayons- Literally means, "Let us try." It is meant with peaceful pursuit or intent. It is spoken proudly between Army combat engineers. It lets us know that we are among likeminded people.

Hooha- This is a battle cry used by the US Army since World War II. It can mean anything but, "NO".

HQ- Head Quarters

Kevlar- This is a soldier's head gear, our helmet. We put it on when we get up in the morning and take it off when we lie down for sleep. It is made of a bullet proof Kevlar material. Mine was adorned with a Playboy Bunny above my right ear.

Knives- Sharp objects used for everything from cutting toenails to putting holes in "Haji." I still have the knife I carried in my right pocket the day that I lost my leg. It dug a nice sized hole there and now skin from my ass covers

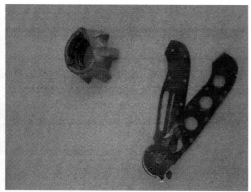

that hole. Also, this is a piece of the RPG that hit me.

M249 SAW-

Mil Spec- Military specification

Mopp Gear- A chemical suit carried by soldiers in case of a toxic chemical attack

Moto knee-

MREs- Meals ready to eat

PMCS- Preventative Maintenance Checks and Service

PT's- Physical training clothing. Sweats

Ruck- A soldier's ruck sack is how he packs and carries clothing and anything else he can fit inside. It is widely debated how to most efficiently pack a ruck sack. I found that rolling clothing before packing and then stuffing them as tight as possible from bottom to top to worked best.

Runners- Running shoes

Show of Force- Simple intimidation. I once fired an AT-4 rocket launcher for what I can tell was "fun".

Test Fire- As far as I could tell, this is what we called it when we wanted to blow something up. Keep in mind that I was a private, so I had a private's understanding.

XT9-

A special thanks to My editor Deb and her husband Gary. They were friends of my dads, they have been helping me through out my entire life, and without them this would not have been possible.

Made in the USA
Lexington, KY
02 December 2019